Tõn

Don't take anything personally

How to be

Tõnn Sarv

Don't take anything personally

Third edition
of the book previously titled
'How to be'

ISBN 9781794664081

Contents

How to become better

No one's perfect. Everyone makes mistakes. It's not that I'm the one and only who's always right and honest, and everyone else is guilty, wrong, a liar and a cheat.

Oh no, I'm sure I've made mistakes too. Surely someone has had to suffer because of me, to be offended, to depend on me and be let down, to endure losses, and perhaps at the time I didn't realise or understand it myself. Who, then, would say such a thing to you in hindsight? Rather, he holds a fist in his pocket and when the opportunity comes, he pays you back.

Yes, it's all about people. You smile and they are smiling, you forgive me and I forgive you, I apologise and they apologise to me.

Well, it sounds good, but it doesn't necessarily get any better if we get better, as everyone finds out at least once in their lifetime. You do good for someone, but there's no way out of it, and maybe you will abused. And so the desire to get better disappears, for what if it doesn't work and nobody cares?

People's rigidity and maliciousness beset us, and this can be mutually grating. It's not going to make any difference, it will just get worse and that's all there is to it, the evil and the rigidity keep deepening.

Yet there are a number of ways to escape from this vicious circle. It is enough just to take the initiative and tone down your own self-sustaining self-justifications. Why should I be right about everything? How can it be that everyone is wrong, but not me?

So, it's enough to admit that I can be stupid about some things; it's a very big step in the right direction.

But what's stopping me? Fear, fright and false pride. As if by only daring to admit I was lost, I would lose something important, lose myself, shatter my peace of mind.

Actually, it is, of course, the opposite. The less we justify ourselves, the more leniently we approach ourselves, the more peaceful we are, and peace of mind comes.

Acknowledging your own mistakes is only the first step. Because if I've been seen to do something wrong once, it's probably happened several times. Not only the doing, but also the undone, the neglected, the lack of attention, even forgetting may be quite a mistake. Cheating on someone's hopes may sometimes be a crime.

You already know how to ask yourself, what's been my greatest mistake or error? Or perhaps the question should be, what's been my worst act, my greatest fault? How many have had to suffer because of me?

You don't have to start looking for self-justifications again, you don't have to have a sense of regret or blame yourself. It's enough to admit it to yourself, to understand that, yes, I was wrong, I did the wrong thing, I caused the suffering. You don't have to stay on your knees, to suffer for it, to blame yourself and to punish, to apologise and to excuse. There's nothing more you can do about it anyway, and you can't change the past.

These are the first steps to getting better: understanding, realisation, recognition. This will lead to a release, and more will follow, and it may eventually go far enough to bring you more confidence, friendliness, love, joy and even happiness.

That's how to become better.

The power of way

We're all on the way, but we're built so we can't see it. We don't know what the future will bring; we can only imagine it, based on our own experiences and memories. Time is moving in only one direction for us, against us. Arrival is only seen when it has already arrived; we only see what is already in hand and over. We know what has been, and on the basis of this knowledge we are also trying to foresee the future and to make good decisions. Alas, mostly it doesn't work.

In the future, things may not be the same as they have been so far. We know that, but yet we believe that perhaps things will still be the same as we are accustomed and adapted to. Just in case, we look at horoscopes and other predictions, not that we really believe them, but still...

Maybe something's changing, maybe something's going to happen, maybe we should do something differently, maybe that's what someone else thinks and we believe them.

And then maybe we'll do something that we wouldn't have otherwise done, change something that might not have been worth the change.

Laozi:

Foresight is a blossom on the way,
But also the beginning of stupidity.

It's like we're sitting in a moving vehicle, but facing backwards. We only see the part of the road that has already passed. We have a steering wheel with which we can change the direction of our movement, of our own free will, but we will still only be able to decide which way to go on the basis of the path we have already travelled, only by the past.

For this purpose, our own experiences, lessons learned and memories count. If our current path in life is more or less smooth, we believe that we can go ahead without much concern, without altering anything, not turning the wheel.

But how do we know that? Maybe there's a road-block in the way, maybe the road will end very soon or turn off somewhere? We can't foresee it and we're going to get a little worried.

Laozi:

Deviation is feared
by whom it seems too easy.

On the contrary, if life seems to be going the wrong way and everything is miserable, we want to start changing something, we start struggling, looking for new directions, rethinking. In fact, both good and bad roads are the same: these are our own perceptions. They don't need to be taken seriously, and there's no need to worry about them.

Laozi:

The least wisdom is enough
to stay on the right way.

Sometimes it seems as though life is hopeless. We are troubled, confused, we misunderstand, every move hurts, everything seems wrong, everything looks bad. But we know there's got to be a good and right way somewhere, and all we need to do is get there.

What to do? Can you hold yourself together quiet-ly until you get out of nowhere, or try to change direction again in the hope that maybe you can get onto an easier path? Nobody knows, but there's always something left.

Laozi:

Way vanish, might remains.

There are many ways: some are longer, some are more obsolete, some are more awkward, some are branching, some go into a thicket. We feel it all on the way. Some of the roads we hardly feel or notice, and some are so troubled that they feel like torture. No way really leads anywhere. The way itself is what is important.

Laozi:

Way is like a stream
that takes the river to the sea.

How do you find the right and good way? How are you going to have the most pleasing life?

Laozi:

Way won't do anything.
And nothing remains undone.

The right ways have a light, very fragile, very simple and very natural draw for us.

Laozi:

Way holds the wayfarer.

It's so delicate that it hardly seems right.

Laozi:

In the right way there is no call.
Yet they are coming.

You can't hear it when you go beserk, rant and rage, and want to get out at any price.

Laozi:

Way has no fight.
Way has no taste.

It may be a secret, but that's how it is: no need to see the way, it can be trusted, you can be released from the wheel.

Laozi:

Calming down is easy to hold.
The unpredictable is easy to do.
Clarity and peace will set up all.

Take the pressure off. The right way may be very close; the right way is easy.

Laozi:

Right way has benefits, no harm.

The missing is useful

There are things that never seem to be enough, that we would still like to have more and more of: sex and money, sweets, chocolate or ice cream, bubble bath and champagne, sea views and luxury yachts, parties with alcohol and drugs, attention and compassion, care and acknowledgement, honour and praise, compliments, forever.

These seem to be the most important things, the highest targets and goals, the ultimate and final happiness to aim for, whether it's money, power, sex or whatever. That all women should want me, all men should adore me.

It's a continuous longing, hunger and thirst, a feeling of everlasting shortage. There's never enough, I will never be satisfied, I still need more and more.

But look at the cactus, for example. It grows between stones and sand, in a hot dry climate with constant water shortage, but it lives and has lived like this for hundreds of millions of years.

Its construction, its tissues and cells, have been shaped just to stay alive despite the dryness. Evaporation is minimal. It can also live for a very long time without any water at all. But if gets some water, it's going to collect it and keep it because it doesn't know when this will happen again.

What kind of life is this, you could ask, with such eternal water scarcity? But just try to 'do good' for the cactus, flood its surroundings with water, and it's going to die. Although water is vital to all living organisms, the cactus cannot survive in that abundance. Its life is constant thirst, constant water shortage, because only in that way can it live.

Some would say it lives in constant suffering. This would sound rather banal to the cactus, but in the human world it has a religious meaning. It's said that life must be suffering. You could think about that.

Why is it that the availability of alcohol and other drugs is limited? Why are there so many restrictions and taboos around sex? Why do the legislative, judicial and executive powers have to be separate and limited? Why can't an official offer any benefits to their relatives and friends? Why is there a lack of money all the time?

The answer, of course, is so we don't die like that cactus in the water. There must be a lack of something for us to be alive; life must be suffering in that sense, and perhaps it would be better if we don't talk about some things, if we forget, or if we don't know something in the first place.

Why do we eat? Because our organism needs nutrients, proteins, carbohydrates or fat? Because we can't live without vitamins, micro-elements or calories? Of course not. We don't really need to eat, at least not as much as we tend to eat, nor do we need to use alcohol or other good stuff.

Eating is not a life-and-death issue, at least not for us, at least not in the world we live in right now. We don't die if we don't eat anything all day, and even a week of starvation won't kill.

And the same goes for all kinds of 'wanting'. We don't have to want everything possible and don't have to worry about anything we don't get. The less we want, the better.

We eat, in particular, to feed our soul. Our soul is hungry, our soul is in trouble, and eating helps, improves our mood, is calming and relieving. In fact, very little food is needed.

The soul needs to feel some taste – salty, bitter, sour, sweet, whatever. He needs to feel something raging under his teeth, he wants something crunchy.

Diet has nothing to do with it. If his chips have become moist and soft, they will no longer be good, although they are still composed of the same nutrients.

Or he wants something relentless or something cold or something bubbling in his mouth. But he only needs it for a moment, and once that moment's gone he doesn't really need it any more.

However, meeting our spiritual needs will trigger metabolic events in our body. Our organism feels like it's starting to be nurtured, and then we're going to keep eating, even though we don't really need it any more. The spiritual necessity, which forced us to crunch the miserable crunchies, was already satisfied, but we munch on and that's how we get fat.

So much eating is not necessary to survive, but we want, we insist, we need to eat all the time because we are sick – our souls are sick, our spirits are sick, we are mentally sick in a serious sense.

If we can't deal with our lives, if we don't know how to live, if we don't get what will help us, if we're sad, afraid, if we hate, if we're jealous, intolerant, offended, then we need a consolation, then we need recognition, justification, support. And that's why we eat – eating helps.

Of course it's a scam, of course it's not a necessity. You won't die if you don't get those chips right now, that ice cream, that chocolate. You're like a little kid. You want it, right now and right here, because it's so important to you, so important that it's all-consuming.

But who makes you consume these things? You're still there with your own soul and your desperation; you're the one who is missing something, and knowing what is missing could be useful.

Laozi:

Wishes bring evil.
Unrest brings trouble.
Wanting brings misery.

Knowing what's enough,
Then that's enough.

Mind the gap

Anyone who has travelled on the London Underground will remember the message repeated from all the loudspeakers on the arrival of a train: 'Mind the gap'.

'Notice the space' between the train and the platform you're stepping on to, that's all. Just a friendly warning, and actually rather over the top because the gap is not very big; you get over it easily, so you don't notice.

But such a warning, especially over a loudspeaker and heard multiple times, remains in the memory as if it was something important. And if you've heard this day by day, year on year, maybe thousands of times in exactly the same manner, it will be especially well remembered.

It's no wonder that this phrase is on T-shirts in the souvenir stores in London, in the titles of albums, films, novels, registered companies, and has been used in lyrics, video games, and so on.

The gap is, in fact, both a 'gap' and 'space', emptiness, something that isn't. And you have a recalling or reminder of this non-existence. Notice the emptiness, notice what isn't. It's pretty deep, isn't it? And not only in the sense that you can step down there accidentally and get hurt. Inevitably, there's more.

What creates music? Sounds? Oh no, the most meaningful parts of music are pauses, silence. As voices become silent, the instruments don't make a sound, the expectation builds..., the tension... If you don't understand it before, at least at the end of the performance, when every sound that was supposed to be sounded has been heard, the moment before the applause... it's the most powerful, the most important moment.

It's all been said, there's nothing left. 'Emptiness', isn't it?

Only then, in this mysterious silence, do you know what it was all about and what everything meant.

Or in art: no miscellaneous objects, whether they three- or two-dimensional, coloured or moving, are important. Well, of course they are, but they are there to give meaning to what is between them, to what is not: the shadows, space, air and emptiness.

Nor in architecture is the meaning in the buildings, houses, walls. Oh no, rather what is between these walls and what is going to happen in these spaces? How it will be to live, work, spend time there, just to be? How will they look, how will you go into them, pass through them? The meaning is in all that is not: rooms, emptiness, hollows and gaps.

Laozi:

Spokes keep the wheel together.
But the hole in the centre
makes it useful.

A vessel is formed from clay.
But the hollow within it
makes it useful.

Or, for example, there is a meeting, council, conference, sitting, presentation. Somebody talks, someone takes notes, and there are settlements, an agenda, moderator, manager, a tight timetable full of events, saturated data, information...

But then there will be a break. And then, during this break time, if nothing formal or matter-of-fact is happening, just at that time, if no one has to do anything any longer, to speak, talk, perform – just then, the most important events happen.

People interact with each other, comment on situations, make jokes, exchange thoughts, realise, understand, reach conclusions and conclude agreements and ties. The room is open, empty and it inspires.

Notice the emptiness.

Mind the gap.

What's important is what isn't.

A very good mind-development practice or meditation is to look at the emptiness, focus on emptiness, wherever we are. We see only what we are looking at, and we look at what has some significance for us, which offers interest. But we can also look in a different way and see other things.

For example, some bushes, a forest, a passage of leaves, branches, stems, where there is nothing interesting. But you can look and discover all that's between them. This empty space, where there is nothing, but where there is air moving, which moves everything, where there are flies, mosquitos, bees, butterflies and birds flying, where the spiders are weaving their webs, the hum of insects and various smells, spreading pollen grains and mushrooms, where leaves and seeds are falling.

Right there, in that emptiness, in that air, is life; it's real, it's exactly that emptiness that unites everyone and everything. You also participate in it with your every breath, breathing in part of it, breathing out your part. You can't live without breathing – no one can – and that's why everyone is in connection through the air, through what you don't even notice.

When we breathe, we smell, and it's not insignificant. All the smells that we cycle through have been sent to someone, come up somewhere, and spread, including those that we may not feel, but that will affect us in one way or another. We are totally defenceless in the face of what we breathe in; we have not the slightest idea of how this affects us, how it changes our lives and decisions, our behaviour, our moves, how the almost unperceived smell can make us want something, do something, move somewhere, get away from somewhere.

But also vice versa. With everything we breathe out, we give the world a signal of what's happening to us, what's in us. Everything in us is flowing in our blood and getting into our lungs and being breathed out of there. We can't hide it. Dogs and many other animals feel and understand our breath. Our loved ones are inhaling what we have breathed out; we are in touch with them, we all are in touch, and the air ocean is a common home for all of us.

And it's not just smells. Through the air, through the same emptiness, voices are spreading. And not only sounds of the woods or the songs of birds, but also sounds with a very clear meaning to us – things people say and the words and phrases we hear – which can make us react in very involuntary ways.

In that same emptiness, the light, which lets us see everything that fills this emptiness, also lets us see the letters that make up the words and statements that have meaning for us, which may again make us react.

There come also touches from the same emptiness. We all feel clothes on our skin all the time, but there are also hugs, handshakes, pats on the shoulder, pokes, kisses, lashes, foot strokes, various tastes, variations of excitement, chills, tickles, desires and more.

All this comes from that place which is not, from the same emptiness that we sometimes notice.

Maybe it's all empty.

Why the truth?

'Not all people need to know all things,' as one of my good friends and companions always loved to say, and this still comes to mind when someone speaks about honesty, frankness, pure spirit of the soul, absolute trust, and things of this nature.

Speaking the truth can cause much more suffering than not speaking. Silence about some things, or even gentle lies, may be much more appropriate and polite.

We know thousands of things that really aren't our business. Someone's birth secret, adoption, the personality of their past intimate partner, someone's serious illness, etc. Sometimes somebody trusts you with secrets, and you have to promise that you won't tell anyone about it. Same story.

But oh, how you would like to share such things. To discuss it with someone and, of course, get the promise that he or she won't tell anyone about it in turn. It's easy to see how secrets spread like that.

The media has, of course, greatly amplified this mentality. The private life of every single person is laid out for all to view and review. Pretty creepy. And the justification is still that people want to know...

Well, maybe that's what they want, but there must be very few things that they necessarily need to know.

Better to live and let others be unaware than burden ourselves and others with unnecessary knowledge. Ripping off the curtain, getting the naked truth may well sell newspapers, but what does it give and where does it lead? We know where it leads: suspicion, distrust, uncertainty.

We need to use knowledge. Useless knowledge only burdens, stirs us up and hurts.

We don't need to know all things, we can't understand everything, and we can't keep up with everything all the time. It's not possible anyway. This is an illusion, a dream, temporary and transient.

Always, something remains unknown, concealed, and it all changes all the time. There is little benefit to such knowledge.

In fact, there are very few things that we really need to know, that need to be understood and considered. You don't need to know how many crimps there are on a beer bottle cap or what is the capital of Burkina Faso or how many ångströms in the wavelength of a yellow line of cadmium. This is useless knowledge to most people.

Nor does it matter what you need to care about or worry about. It doesn't matter what you need to have, what you want or achieve. You don't have to find out who you really are, what your destiny is or who you might have been in a previous life, what your special qualities are or where you really belong. These are questions of faith, perceptions, wishes and desires; they all arise from self-importance, wanting to be somehow special, necessary and right. We can live, we don't have to worry. There's one life, to live.

This is all fine, but surely there are people who also need some secret knowledge, who believe that things are not all the way they seem, that in fact there are conspiracies and secret observers and that we are only being manipulated and lied to. That's how you get really nervous.

'What is truth?' retorted Pilate. (John 18:38)

Yes, sometimes you're lied to, but you're going to listen to it, smile and maybe lie back. You both know that it's not true, but it has yet to be reconciled and settled. That's the way it is, it's a courtesy that doesn't cost anything. Whatever they say, whatever it looks like, just smile.

The truth may be somewhere, but it's not being investigated; knowledge of it is no use, and it's not possible to know everything, to understand everything.

Some talk about the arrival of a post-truth era. Why not? Maybe someday we will regard the seekers of final truths with the same kind of amusement as we now look at believers in fairy tales.

You don't have to do anything; you don't need anything. Not everything can be found out; it doesn't all have to be understood. Rather, you may gradually get rid of excessive things, desires and thoughts. You can forget the useless knowledge and the old beliefs. You can let them go and be free.

You don't have to have anything or anyone – you don't have to be anyone at all.

Where you look, that's where you go

Remember how you learn to ride a bicycle? You turn the handlebars too hard at first, before you can begin to steer it, more or less.

But then there is a new problem – you keep riding into the holes and the edge of the road where you don't want to go.

And why? Because you don't want to ride into the holes – you're afraid of them and that's why you're staring at them. But where you look, that's where you go.

We are all afraid sometimes, and sometimes very afraid. We often don't like a lot of things. At the same time, we also like a lot of other things, we want a lot of things, we desire, we want, we believe, we hope. And we are saddened because we can't get these pleasant things, or they don't come to us. We tend to come up with the bad things we're afraid of.

And why? Because we're looking at more of those things we don't like, the things we're afraid of, whatever's irritating us, and so we run into them.

You drive where you look – that's how simple it is. What you're thinking about, that's what you get; what you're afraid of is coming.

To the healer comes the one who is not well, who is broken or at least thinks he is broken. If you admit that you're not okay, you're not. To the smart comes the one who isn't smart, who's stupid or at least thinks he's stupid. If you admit you're not smart, you aren't.

Who can fix your brokenness or get you out of stupidity?

No one. They can only help you to find out that you're not broken, that you're not stupid.

Nor did Jesus exacerbate the paralysis. Oh no, he said:

'Get up! Pick up your mat and walk.' (John 5:8)

Every living being can be a God, Guru or Master. The more we love them, the more of them we find. Nothing else is needed!

J. Lennon: *All You Need Is Love.*

Don't you know that you yourselves are God's temple and that God's Spirit dwells in your midst? (1 Corinthians 3:16)

Truly I tell you, whatever you did for one of the least of these brothers and sisters of mine, you did for me. (Matthew 25:40)

Whatever happens, it's going to happen to you; whatever you think about it, that's what's happening right now, at this very moment. No one and nothing is separate, before or after; everything is now, here and now, there is nothing more.

In that sense, it doesn't matter if you suffer or somebody suffers because of you, whether you get hurt or you hurt. If you hurt somebody, you make someone suffer, you suffer and you get hurt. And similarly, your suffering and pain are everyone's pain and suffering. Everything that is done to you is done to anyone; you are not the only one, you are not special.

J. Donne: *And therefore never send to know for whom the bell tolls; it tolls for thee...*

God is talking to us or through us. Or we speak to Him or through Him, because of Him. It doesn't matter, because we're all one, both with Him and with all of us together, you and me, us and them. Pick up the rock – there you are. Chop the log in half – there He is.

You can't breathe in all the time and you can't live all the time; sometimes you've got to die. You can't die if you haven't lived and you can't live if you don't die. We don't need to think we're much smarter than anyone. Let everyone deal with their own issues; no need to think that someone is sick or foolish, and needs treatment or teaching.

If anybody asks, advice may be given as to which path would be right or better suited, but this is just advice and recommendations, nothing more. No need to prohibit or to order, no need to promise anything. We can't afford to do so. It is better to fulfil the promises before we give them.

You mustn't think that anyone else is any better or smarter or more important. Knowledge is abundant, opinions are many, the means are plentiful – some are functional, some are not, some are beneficial, some are not. So what? Everything can be, everything can, but nothing needs to be done.

A person may be smart and healthy in nature, but he can think himself stupid and sick. You're not who you were a year ago or ten years ago – you changed. What mattered to you may no longer fit. And the other way around: for the one you were suited to yesterday, you may no longer be right or necessary today.

No one can be blamed for the change; what is important is how we can or can't go with the changes, continue to be consistent with them, adapt to them, harmonise. Better still, be better – that counts.

This can also be described in other ways. We talk about waves, vibration, oscillations, energy levels, tuning and, yes, it's the same thing. Still, there is a need to reset; still, there is a need to go with the changes and change yourself, all the time. There is nothing permanent, nor can there be.

Why complain and offend because of how something has changed and is no longer what it should be like? Why should something be just the way you remember? What does it matter?

These are misunderstandings that arise between the moving and the stationary, friction that fires up the passion, drives up the heat.

And here comes the need to fit, to set up, to be in line again, to be better. Not to fear or despise, but to look where you want to get to.

You don't have to hold on, you can let go.

But how?

This is a good question and here comes a good suggestion:

Be calm.

That doesn't mean you should be happy with everything. That doesn't mean you should let all things happen. You're calm if you don't get involved in everything that's going on. If you don't judge or compare, if you don't fear or want anything, if you don't hold anything in contempt.

You are the one feeling your contempt, pain and suffering. Peace can only be in you.

It's the only thing you can achieve, the only thing you can feel. As for others, you don't know anything; others can't be influenced, others don't matter, the only thing that counts is your peace.

Stay calm. It's very important. Don't be afraid, don't worry, look where you want to get to.

Where you look, that's where you go.

But that's not all

If anything can be called 'reality', maybe it's just what you see at this moment, what you hear, feel, right now. Everything else you've seen, heard and experienced before, what you've thought or considered, what you've been told or shown, or what you've read, is no longer a 'reality', but just your memories of something. Your dreams, intentions and plans aren't a reality. Nor do all your wishes, desires, deliberations, views, opinions or assessments have anything to do with reality.

What could be called reality is also limited to the extent of your own vision, hearing and sensation at this moment. Every time you move your eyes, the 'reality' changes. And you only see and only hear whatever is important to you at this moment, with some point for you, with some kind of meaning.

Hundreds of billions of creatures see, hear and feel different 'realities' at the same moment, and yours is only one of these and cannot be more real or more acceptable.

What gives you the assurance that your reality is the only one or the right and proper one? The reality that your friend is wrong about, that your neighbour doesn't understand. Don't forget about your baby or your cat.

How is your reality somehow better or more righteous than your cat's? Your cat doesn't worry about it, he just is, he has no illusions, he doesn't pretend. Yet he thinks and he has consciousness.

Words, thoughts, assessments, opinions, perceptions, illusions are what make us unhappy. But what do the world's wisest teachers recommend?

Free yourself from illusions, free yourself from opinions and assessments, from words and names. Don't worry, don't bother, live in the moment.

All that's happening, and everything that comes is right and useful and valuable for you.

There's no need to fight or to resist, to question, to riot or to do anything. Be calm, comfortable and at peace. The way it seems to you is how it is. Be thankful, take it, accept it and be happy.

But you think you know, and that what you know is real, that it's right and true. Maybe you even think you should fight for it, so everyone else knows the same way and gets to know what you know?

Where have you picked this up, how has this crazy idea come to you? How can you be so sure?

You've built yourself a fortress that is you. You know, you think, and that's all you've got: your ego, your 'me'. If you didn't have that confidence, you'd go crazy, if your mind had to lose the only support it has, the only link to the so-called reality in which it thinks it is acting.

This anchor, this self-censorship, this confidence, this egotism, as some might say, is needed. It holds life and helps us live, it helps us to cope, to act and to achieve.

You've done all this, you're the ultimate reality, pure truth.

Nothing has any meaning or value or sense, if we have not yet assigned these meanings and values to something, if we have not yet committed ourselves to it.

A short study of consciousness

We cannot define ourselves, our mind or our consciousness. These things can only be described by comparisons or metaphors.

Your consciousness is not you. Consciousness is an environment in which the mind can appear, or a better way to say it is that consciousness is the environment you appear in.

Consciousness is a tool, a function, like a field, a potential. It's like a water surface, able to make waves. In terms of consciousness, we feel waves as movements in the mind.

Its waves can form temporary or persistent shapes and patterns. These become what we consider to be ourselves, our personality or whatever.

These shapes and patterns are formed by various sensations, perceptions and images which enter into the mind through the mind's doors or are created by the mind itself. This means everything we see, hear, read, feel, smell and think, all the time.

These are all the things that 'happen'. They're like winds that make waves in the water.

There are moving waves, regular waves, constant waves moving in the same direction, circular waves coming from one point, those that rise up and break, the surf and the ripples, the foam and white horses, storms and hurricanes.

There are also standing waves that take a more definite shape and form, and which can persist for quite a long time. As conceptions, they may be called beliefs, principles, definite attitudes or world views, which altogether may also be considered as the personality.

All of them are caused by something and all these causes may also change, but our behaviour, opinions, expressions and actions will come from precisely these causes.

We already have long-established habitual behaviours and actions, like walking, breathing, eating, excretion, sleeping, etc., which have become just part of everyday life, so normal we hardly notice them.

Only if conditions change – if we are being prevented from doing something or if we are offered other options, if new reasons arise – then we start to notice more again. Something more to learn, something new to take into account. Typically, this happens when travelling, hiking, seeing new places, meeting new people, dealing with new relationships and circumstances for example.

Surprises may appear. Some unexpected wind trap, some unexpected event may also create a totally unprecedented outburst, or motivate us to express ourselves or act in a totally different way. And then we might be surprised: 'I didn't know I could be so disgusting,' for example.

And afterwards, we realise that a human being is still a great mystery.

We can do everything. It's all possible. Our capabilities are virtually unlimited. The question is just whether and how we know and feel these possibilities, how we use them. Our consciousness is extremely flexible, fluid and adaptable. The occasional strong wind may cause special patterns on the water surface, but we will still be able to achieve a wide variety of specialised capabilities and skills, such as speaking and understanding language, and many more.

It may be very likely that we don't understand or recognise many of the possibilities of consciousness, not yet having begun to use them. One of the greatest opportunities is probably to experience pure consciousness, which is not disturbed by any reflection of the mind, when the mind is fully silent. It's like a plain field, a perfectly reflective water surface, a pure land where everything is possible. Achieving this state of consciousness is entirely possible.

Consciousness can be in different states. Every comparison will fail, but we will still stick to the water metaphor.

Normal water is like water always is, familiar and basic. And, similarly, our normal everyday consciousness is the most familiar and normal state of consciousness for us. Just as water characteristics may change if contaminants are added or if the pressure or temperature differs from the norm, so the state of our consciousness may also change.

We may 'lose consciousness', we may faint, we may sleep and have dreams. We may become hypnotised. The conditions of consciousness may also, to some extent, be affected by very small quantities of different odours, substances or perceptions. A cup of coffee, a music track or a glass of wine may send us into a different state. Much more powerful, of course, are the effects of larger quantities and stronger active substances.

Consciousness may also be altered by the mind's own functioning, contingent on mood. You can make yourself angry, sad or happy just by thinking about yourself. You can make yourself anxious, start worrying, complaining or be troubled.

The question, again, is how we can control these conditions, how we can govern and manage these movements of thought and emotions.

But come back to the basics. Consciousness is the environment, the way or the field in which the mind appears and moves. As waves consist of water, so the mind is made up of consciousness.

Consciousness cannot be tasted or felt, it simply is. The mind is movements of consciousness – thoughts, imagination, feelings, moods, concepts and other conscious activities.

All the movements of consciousness are caused by the signals coming into the mind through the doors of the mind – hearing, touching, seeing, tasting, smelling – or from the mind itself – thoughts, memories, imaginings, delusions, etc.

The more persistent shapes and patterns of the mind are called principles, opinions, beliefs, attitudes, assessments and views, and together they also form what we consider to be the personality, or ourselves.

It is clear that neither waves nor clouds have any meaning, any purpose or aim. They only arise and disappear, come and go, according to how the winds are blowing, according to different conditions. Nor is there any sense or meaning in anyone's moods or feelings. These are caused by similar random events. Yes, they can be noticed and recognised. And they may also leave again, just like any clouds or ripples. These are all just delusions, empty of any meaning, random reflections, blurred and temporary.

And as there is no point or meaning in your feelings or moods, there is no point or meaning in the more lasting shapes and forms that consist of these moods or feelings: your opinions, assessments, attitudes, etc. They arise from the conditions, from the mutual connections that the mind delights in creating between various sensations, perceptions and thoughts. They are called generalisations, conclusions, views, opinions, beliefs, ideals, principles, etc.

If you have experienced or heard of some sort of incident with someone, you would expect, hope for or fear similar events under similar conditions in the future. It's pretty natural.

Unfortunately, the scope and understanding of our perceptions are quite limited. We have nothing else to use but our sensations and perceptions that come through the doors of the mind, in addition to past experiences and memories, thoughts and imagination. We have nothing else but these limited tools. It is like sitting in a dark room where we can only look out through a tiny slot. We only see a tiny piece of everything, and just for a moment.

If we hear, read or see something that is not consistent with our experience and knowledge, we often don't notice it at all. We don't recognise it, can't grasp it, and we just have no idea what to think about it. Or we become irritated and immediately engage in a fight. How can it be that someone looks different from me? Thinks differently? Believes in another way? We've identified ourselves with our perceptions, delusions, opinions and imagination. We are prepared to die for our principles and beliefs or even kill somebody.

Of course, there are other options. We can learn something from new events and phenomena, and thus develop. We can let go of our current opinions and attitudes, and change. We can start to understand that we can't even be sure of ourselves. We can just notice these new things, just take note and nothing more.

All our decisions, all our activities, all the things we say are based only on this brief moment, in a limited area, only on our own experiences and conclusions. And even worse, we constantly forget what we have seen and experienced. We remember selectively and incorrectly, we believe in the fiction, we are afraid, we hope and spend a lot of time in our imagination.

Yet we consider it real, final and determined. It is our self-consciousness, our confidence and sometimes self-esteem. We consider it all to be self-owned, to be ours, to be ourselves.

Some say the mind is the only reality and the only truth.

Story of geese

A story, based on an ancient magical folk song.

Others were given different work, but you got a simple task – to keep the chickens, geese and ducks, and take care of their wings and feathers. Keep your peace of mind, make sure it doesn't go away, that the birds don't rise in flight, don't escape and fly away. What could be easier?

L. Carroll:

'Come back!' the Caterpillar called after her. 'I've something important to say!'

This sounded promising, certainly: Alice turned and came back again.

'Keep your temper,' said the Caterpillar.

But the mind is unsettled, still looking for something, still wanting something else, something new, something more interesting. And it starts to do something, to create, weave, cheer and build, without even understanding.

And there awake these unexpected feelings and storms, the thunderstorms that scare geese from the field and ducks from the meadow.

W. Shakespeare:

Lo as a careful housewife runs to catch,
One of her feathered creatures broke away,
Sets down her babe and makes all swift dispatch
In pursuit of the thing she would have stay:

Whilst her neglected child holds her in chase,
Cries to catch her whose busy care is bent,
To follow that which flies before her face:
Not prizing her poor infant's discontent;

So run'st thou after that which flies from thee,
Whilst I thy babe chase thee afar behind,
But if thou catch thy hope turn back to me:
And play the mother's part, kiss me, be kind.

So will I pray that thou mayst have thy Will,
If thou turn back and my loud crying still.

What to do? Peace of mind has gone flying. Nothing is the same any more: anxiety has taken hold.

A simple task – take care of the chickens, hold the geese and mind the ducks – proved to be insurmountable.

What can be done other than crying at home? Start at the source, start with the data, with the reasons, where the task came from and where everything began, and from there, very carefully remember what went wrong, how it was lost.

A mind journey should be taken. No one else can do this for you; no one else is interested in bringing back your mind.

Equip and prepare yourself. It may not be easy. In particular, keep your patience, which is needed most of all.

Wherever you go, you will find yourself, in your own nature, in your own depths, to your own birth and death, hell and paradise.

And then you ask: What is all this? Where I am going? What I am looking for? Who I am?

But no one is answering you. No one can hear you.

Nothing's gone away. You're there and there isn't anything missing, but you don't see it, can't hear it, and it feels like you're missing something.

There are a lot of teachings and teachers, recommendations, advisers and guides. But they all repeat one and the same message: all roads lead to purpose and no road really leads anywhere.

You're already there, only you don't know that, you don't recognise yourself yet.

'A challenge,' the hare suggests to the snail, 'which one will come home first?'

'Okay,' says the snail and pulls himself into his house.

You lost something important. You lost reality, it flew away, and now you're upset. Now you're looking for it, trying to find it again, but you can't. Seeking something is what stops you seeing, hearing, understanding or finding out about it.

You fell asleep and you haven't woken up yet. It's still a dream, it's just that goose story you're telling yourself, singing to yourself, and you can't shut up.

You lost your soul, your clarity of mind, your real being, real knowledge. You only see what you can imagine, what you think and understand, what you think you want, only what's important and has meaning to you.

It seemed so simple, so easy – to keep and protect the winged and feathered birds, just to look at them as they are, in a natural way, letting them be, freely. Such an intriguing thing, such an easy task – keep your temper.

'Is that all?' said Alice, swallowing down her anger as well as she could.

'No,' said the Caterpillar.

Keeping your temper is, of course, important, but no, that's not all. It is only now that your pure, undisturbed and peaceful mind has flown away, that it has become valuable and necessary.

So was it worth it, so you could do something, bind your self, find something else to want and achieve?

Now you see what your geese and ducks were worth. They weren't yours; you only had to watch them, keep them in mind, but now they're gone and now it's your problem – how to get them back.

They have become yours, your wishes and your dreams.

But now you can quietly start to realise that you haven't really lost anything, you aren't missing anything, that you still have everything, including all those winged and feathered creatures. You took them and now you're with them, much more so than when you only had to watch them.

And you know where they flew, where they went. You see the gate, you see the door, but you can't enter yet. There is no clarity, no courage and no certainty.

You're starting to realise that it was not the geese that were the ones you had to watch and take care of. That keeping and caring itself was important, you were important, the story was all about you.

And then, finally, you go in, to yourself, where the door has been opened and the gate unlocked. Because now you're ready for this, your mind is ripe for it, because now you know what you're doing, you're no longer worried, no longer afraid.

All of your mind, all your geese and ducks are growing and maturing. You can support yourself on their bones, taste their meat, drink their blood. These are your bones, which have now become strong; it's your flesh that has now matured and it's your blood that is now foaming like beer.

They can no longer fly apart; no longer can they dissipate or disappear; no longer will they return to old manners or habits. Everything's changed, you're sure, you're strong.

The fight is over, the search is over. No more loss or victory, no searching or finding. You're serene and fulfilled at last. Nothing can dissolve you or mislead you any more. You've reached home, in your heart, in your centre, you're fully present in yourself now, and you're for real.

You don't need these goose-ducks any more, these winged and feathered things. They took you there and they brought you home.

You don't need to guard them any more, take care of them, keep them or protect them; you're with them now, you're in them; they're gone now, and everything is very sure, clear and real.

There are no differences; everyone has become one. There is no more you and others; everything is one, you and all, and this experience can grow into something very big. You know everything now, you see everything, and nothing's hidden from you any more.

And you can start to feel like you're now really big, super big, so big you reach the clouds, so tall you can look down on everything. You're full of yourself and it's terrible.

You're strong now, super strong, overly strong, you can do so much and get it done and you're therefore truly dangerous, scarily so. Even standing still, even if you don't do anything, don't think about anything, don't intend anything.

Now you have to get rid of it; now you have to get rid of yourself, you have to turn to a real beginning or origin, to the source, and to grow.

They were all just your imaginings that you were trying to monitor and watch. Now there are no more of them, you're one with them, no matter.

Now you need someone to bring you back down to the ground. You can be useful now.

Three old men

There is a famous picture of three old men tasting a large bowl of vinegar. One thinks it's too sour, in another's opinion it's quite bitter, but for the third one it seems pretty sweet. There is only one and the same substance, one and the same phenomenon, one and the same life, but it seems so different to each of the three people.

These three old men are the well known, wise teachers Confucius, Buddha and Laozi. It's very unlikely the three of them got together like this, although they all lived in the same era, around 2,500 years ago.

Their teachings, at least in China, have been equally and highly honoured, so some even talk of Chinese synergy or syncretism, in which they are blended together.

A Chinese person could call himself a Confucian, a Buddhist and also a Taoist, without seeing any contradiction. Perhaps, they might say: born as a Taoist, living as a Confucian and dying as a Buddhist.

In fact, these teachings are quite different and, in some respects, they contradict each other.

Confucianism, for instance, considers a person bad in terms of his nature and teaches how he should be educated, developed and improved. In Buddhism, human nature is considered good (each one has Buddhahood!) and people are taught how to get rid of obstacles, defilements and suffering. In Taoism, however, the natural course of things should be followed.

These three teachings are all quite understandable. Whether human nature is good or bad is of course a matter for assessment, which is known to be subjective and biased. But it is also clear that without care and cultivation, without restrictions and development, the 'right' person cannot manifest. A newborn baby hasn't even started walking on two feet, not to mention talking or thinking.

Thus, the human nature of a man or woman can only emerge through the involvement of other people, through culture – and it's hard to be considered human without culture in particular. Another question, of course, is whether and how to assess various cultures, manners, practices and values. What should be considered as noble and humane and what as 'sour'?

And, of course, human nature can also be thought of as essentially good and pure, clear and transparent, and that it is the involvement of other people, through culture, that brings false thoughts and prejudices, assessments and attitudes that stop us understanding the way things are. People start wanting or despising, preferring or avoiding. Various defilements arise. The importance of self-differentiation emerges and a mistaken idea of personality develops.

True, this addictive chain can be interrupted, by studying and practising awareness to see things as they are without meaning and importance: they are empty. Without such enlightenment, however, ultimately misery and unpleasantness, distress and 'bitter' suffering will be experienced.

It is also possible for anyone to let their mind and nature remain free and innocent, sincere and clear, seeing and feeling everything freely and calmly from the beginning. Letting all go along the way, of course, without acting. Teaching without words, without commands, leaving everything that is superfluous, useless and void; being unwilling to compete or fight, especially with other people; feeling natural, with simplicity and clarity of 'sweetness'.

Obviously, the human race still seems too young to reach a consensus on their own culture at the most general level. There seem to be only two things that all people agree on: using two legs for walking, and using sign systems for communication or talking. In terms of everything else, particularly how to raise children, how to have sex, how and what to eat or how to cover own bodies, there have been always endlessly differing opinions, manners and beliefs.

Fair play and good will

First of all, we must agree on the rules.

This is what society expects and demands: that there are rules, laws that are valid, a framework that everyone recognises and within which everything can function. Obviously, there are rules, practices and manners in nature, among fishes, birds, insects and other animals, too.

The rules are sacred. They cannot be changed, they cannot be contested, we have to live by them. Anyone trying to change them or to live according to different rules is dangerous, because that's a violation of an honest game.

Laozi:

Nobody can ignore the customs.
Attack will follow immediately.

There must be rules in the game. It is not possible to play chess or football without knowing and taking account of the rules. The question then comes up as to whether life and being in general is a game or something else, whether, as in sports, there are some rules of the game for living and being, things we need to consider.

Life and being in general is not a game or a competition, but various games and competitions can teach us a lot about life.

There are rules, regulations and laws, but there is also goodwill and an honest game. Fair play means, among other things, that you will not take advantage of an accident or a mistake by the opponent even if the rules allow it. There are always unwritten rules alongside the main rules and they will also be well known. Don't go on a golf course, for example, with a hat that says, 'Buy Volvo' on it, because it's just something you don't do.

In an educational sense, sport and games have played a very important role in the Western world for over a century.

The development of the physical body is of course essential; it is also necessary to develop skill, accuracy, decision-making, speed, attention and flexibility, to learn and use these capabilities in good and fair ways. Of course, sport develops self-confidence and much more.

However, this subject also has a much wider importance. Thus, the qualities of persistence, patience, accountability, dignity, playing an honest game, loyalty, cooperation, governance, subordination, respect for the rules and many more are necessary and essential, especially in the field of ethics.

'It's just not cricket,' says the Englishman, if he wants to draw attention to fraud. The game is sacred; the game has its own spirit; the game is a model of life.

The handicap – improving the chances of the weaker players – has been written into the rules of several sports. So, to make the game more interesting, and to make sure we also make the same concessions in real life, we provide support and protection, give up our advantages of strength and many other things.

Respect – for rules, judges and opponents – is the foundation of the sporting world and also the foundation of Western civilisation.

The laws must be followed and the representatives of power must be obeyed. The competitors have to be respected. If you can't do this in the game, how are you going to do it in real life?

Withstanding a loss is also a skill that can be learned through sports.

It was just a game. Whoever won or lost is not so important after all. More important is the pleasure of a beautiful game. The opponents thank each other for a good game.

If someone starts blaming someone else after their loss and arguing, they are a bad loser. And when someone starts bragging about their victory and taunting their opponents, they don't know how to win.

It depends on the question

Language is a scourge and a blessing at the same time. It seems to us that if we have already named or labelled something, there can still be all kinds of questions about it. Alas, these questions may not always have answers. It depends on the question.

In mathematics, a beautiful concept is used – uncertainty. It is not possible to say, for example, what the result will be when something is divided by zero, because it is indefinite: there is no answer. If this has happened accidentally or inconspicuously, one cannot trust the result or answer to be correct or reasonable. After dividing by zero, anything can be 'proved', and similar uncertainties arise when infinity is involved. Zero and infinity should be treated with great caution; when they are used it's easy to reach very strange conclusions.

And similarly, there are also wrongly asked questions. We cannot ask what is the purpose of life or whether God exists or what is the truth. These are uncertainties, empty questions. But they can easily be given content and definition by asking:

Why do you live? What's the point of your life? What do you expect from life? What are you sure about?

Because these questions can only have personal answers. There is no sense of life without a living entity, nor God without God's admirer. A man himself gives his life a reason and a purpose. In the same way, everyone creates their own God: all of it comes from the inside.

It is easy to see how this also applies to love or happiness.

But it's especially interesting when we have already figured something out and then we ask what it is. The answer cannot be that it's a fiction or that it doesn't mean anything.

'The truth' or 'God' may be somehow 'there', but these concepts are what we've created and figured out; yet we don't really know what they're supposed to mean.

Let the truth be as it is, or as it seems to be, but there are some definite, undeniable facts, and some of these are also important. Important facts are important indeed and they can also be called truths or even noble truths. (Why not? The idea remains the same.) But there are important facts that can be understood and kept in mind. Things that don't change or disappear, that affect us all the time, that we are constantly dealing with and can't deny.

There aren't many of these important facts, and they are very simple:

- *There are inconveniences in life*
- *There is a reason*
- *You can get rid of this reason*
- *There is a method for that.*

We will now have a closer look at them.

There are inconveniences in life

Who could doubt this fact? There are always inconveniences: rain is falling, a child is pouting, the wife's
complaining, there's too little money, his head hurts, her
stomach is empty, no one calls, annoying noises, horrible fatigue, enforced waiting, and so the anxiety begins...

It's not that these things cause us much trauma,
torment or suffering; some may not even be things we
particularly dislike, nor are they great or serious events.

In fact, there is no need to worry about things like
this; they come and go, and some remain longer than
others. They just need to be considered; they can of
course be dealt with. Meanwhile, take care of your
health, build your career, develop skills and abilities, be
calm and joyful in every situation.

In fact, most of our problems and inconveniences
are fairly normal, totally natural things to experience
constantly, throughout life. They are still unpleasant, still
undesirable and unsatisfactory, but they can be noticed
and they can be our teachers.

We're dealing with them all the time. We wipe out
the irritating dust particle, turn to the other side while
sleeping, move away from the noise or disgusting smell,
scratch the itchy spot, sip something, wave away the fly
or mosquito. We still want to get rid of suffering, inconvenience, annoyances.

There is nothing special or mystical about it: this is
our daily life, our everyday activity. We have no need to
achieve anything or get anywhere with these actions.
Rather, we want to get rid of something, avoid, remove
or lose something; we just want to change the existing
situation that has caused us displeasure or dissatisfaction.

But we still don't feel satisfied. The dissatisfaction,
the discontentment has somehow been embraced and
become inevitable. We have been taught and raised to
wait and suffer.

First of all, the child has to learn to cope with their own needs, to suppress those which are not acceptable to those around them, and learn that they must grow up and change.

Then there is always something else to be achieved, somewhere to get to before we can begin to hope or wish for anything. As if it's not yet real life, but some sort of preparation for something you have to reach in the future.

And not just in your education and career. You are told you must not be satisfied with your appearance, your pay, your position, you must be lacking something all the time.

Repeatedly, you will be told what you do wrong and what you have misunderstood, that you still have to find the most important things for yourself, the main events, the right people: your life, your calling, your true self, your soulmate.

Constantly, you are taught how to be calm, relax and deal with stress, concerns and tensions as if the they were perfectly natural and normal states of mind. But you can't see it anyway, you can't understand it, because everyday worries and tensions and stress don't let you feel free, calm or relaxed.

Such contradictory recommendations and teachings, if you pay attention to them and take them seriously, are rather disruptive and are really not going to let you see anything very clearly or understand anything properly. But within them we live.

And so we are never totally satisfied with the existing situation and we would like to change it somehow, and in that sense there may indeed be truth in the saying that life is suffering, no matter how trivial it may sound. Especially if we notice that mostly we are just dealing with changing and improving our existing situation.

The unpleasantness, the inconvenience, also arises if something changes, if it is no longer what it used to be.

All the time, you knew, believed, felt, and could count on it. You were sure of it, but now it's not the same any more.

It may have been your favourite coffee shop or bus route, street, bench or tree, a view or service you particularly liked, the price or value of something that changed with no warning, something that was re-designed in a way you had never seen or considered possible. It may have been someone familiar or close to you who did or said something that startled you, which you wouldn't have expected from them. It may have been your favourite singer, or an actor, a politician, a celebrity, who surprised you in an unpleasant way.

It may not be much that changes. But every time it turns out that something is not same as you had previously known or thought, expected or determined, you feel immediately disturbed. You feel like you've been let down, betrayed. You feel insulted and you suffer for it.

It may also be unpleasant for you to suffer for what you've done yourself. Shame and embarrassment in hindsight. You're sorry, and you feel guilty. Or regret because you let some good opportunity go to waste. Or you're worried about what might come.

Open any newspaper or news portal and what do you see? People win or lose elections, prices may rise or fall, a virus or epidemic may start spreading, harmful substances may be released, all kinds of threats and warnings of things that can all happen. There may be an apology and compensation for some injustice, it may seem necessary to seek revenge. What might have been if something had gone differently? The mystery of a ship or fallen aircraft that disappeared is still unsolved. Somewhere, a big accident has happened, someone's secrets are coming to light, some people are still getting very large sums of money for nothing.

It can also be unpleasant, even offensive, to see, hear or read something that doesn't suit your convictions and principles. The behaviour of all kinds of unpleasant and stupid people can be unbearable, especially when they bother you or you have to be near them.

Unpleasant feelings also come up if something doesn't go as you hoped or how it was promised. You spent the money, you made the effort, you trusted, believed, contributed, waited – but nothing. Things like that can make you very angry.

But the most unpleasant and intolerable of all is if you aren't recognised, if people don't trust you. If you are suspected, accused, or people lie to your face, you will feel deceived and betrayed. Or if you're smirked at in public, insulted or humiliated.

All this can be totally unbearable. And if it goes on all the time, day after day, for a lifetime, then it is easy to reach the conclusion that life is suffering...

Is there a reason for all this?

There is a reason

But now we're reaching the point where we should stop and consider whether there is any need at all to go ahead, talk more about this, whether there is more to know. Maybe we shouldn't.

This book may have already caused offence; from here on, it may start to cause resentment, because the story is gets much more personal.

In fact, it has already done so, because these dislikes, problems and suffering are already personal and arose perhaps because you took them personally.

Maybe you are the reason for all your inconvenience and suffering, or rather who you're imagining yourself to be.

The one who suffers, who is not satisfied, who has to tolerate inconvenience is you, it's yourself. You suffer, you're not satisfied, you feel uncomfortable.

Actually, it's your image of yourself in your own imagination, it's who you think you are – that is who suffers.

Still you say *I, me, mine, my, with me...* Actually, it's not all going to happen to you – it's not all about you anyway. Whoever you think you are doesn't matter at all.

Every conflict, every anger, every strong reaction always starts with someone, some person who feels wounded, insulted, badly treated.

W. Shakespeare:

Then hate me when thou wilt; if ever, now;
Now, while the world is bent my deeds to cross...

This is an example of someone overestimating themselves. In reality, nobody is against him, no one hates him – it just seems so to him, it's just his own image of himself. But he suffers for it.

It's all affection, bonds, addiction and connection, personal hate and feeling hatred, nerve and nervousness; our 'selves' have been connected and tied to all of this. It's all just personal need, the desire and the wish, the inconvenience and the suffering.

You may suffer because your last picture or post didn't get enough likes, you haven't received enough recognition.

Of course, there is a certain anxiety behind it, an uncertainty, cowardice, weakness; it is the need to get rewarded, it is dependence on rewards to feel more confident, more courageous and stronger again.

But who needs them, who depends on them? You're the one, who else is there?

What do they think? How do I look? What are they saying about me? Do they get me wrong? Don't I give a weird impression? Did I get noticed?

All the trouble starts from something taken personally, from not being indifferent, not being in one-allness, all-oneness.

If no one agrees with your views, it doesn't mean they hate you. And you have no reason to hate them. You are not your point of view, opinion or position.

These are totally different things. There is no need to hold them, to identify yourself with them, to take them personally or be offended because of them.

All you see, hear or read is nothing to do with you. You see something, you hear, read, feel, understand – all right, but it doesn't touch you, it's not done to you.

Even what they say to you or what kind of relations they have with you is not about you, but only their words or attitudes.

Ultimately the most offensive questions are these:

How does that suit me? How do I like that? Why would I care? What does that mean for me? What can I get for that?

These are the most shocking, the most selfish questions and if one can't begin to think in a different way, if these remain the final questions, if there are no more questions, then there is nothing more to talk about, there is nowhere to go, there is no way to help.

As if nothing else existed, as if the whole world revolved around you, the most important person here, as if your thoughts, deliberations and attitudes were significant or even the most important things that everyone else must take notice of.

But surely it's all as it seems to me, is there anything else? Only I am real, only what I feel is right...?

Actually, it doesn't matter what you think or imagine, nobody cares. Everyone has their own opinions and thoughts and they are much more important to them than yours.

All the trouble begins with the importance of self-differentiation, putting yourself at the centre of the world, of your imagination, as if you should matter to everyone.

And even if someone approaches you and tells you something specific about yourself, you don't need to let it bother you. Maybe someone doesn't like your appearance, someone reviews your speech or behaviour, someone praises you for something, someone's thrilled about you.

It's their business and it doesn't have to hurt you in any way. Your appearance, your suit or dress or hair isn't you. Whatever you've done or said or written, it's not you. It's a matter for others, how they deal with your appearance, your words, your being and how you do things; think about it, and appreciate it, but it shouldn't bother you.

Are the birds singing about you? Does the wind blow because of you? Of course not. So then, why should someone's opinion or attitude be your business? What kind of relationship are you supposed to have with that?

Any addiction and connection, any association with yourself will make you unhappy.

Nor do we need much else in this human world if our existence is at least recognised. There may not be anything else, but if you're just ignored, if nobody cares, if you don't even get noticed, it can still hurt, it can make you angry...

Actually, this is a very natural human response. Even the most humble beggar monk would rejoice if he could somehow be invaluable or necessary. You can still enjoy it, but you don't have to involve yourself, to make yourself more important, to depend on it.

The cat won't be insulted if somebody steps over him without noticing; the cat doesn't need to feel necessary, he doesn't need recognition. But the human being wants to feel needed; it's almost as important to them as food, air or water. A man may starve in order to gain recognition, hold his breath, be thirsty in the desert. He may even commit crimes for that.

Recognition gives us the confidence we need, and if we don't have enough of it, we'll imagine it.

You, yourself

The trouble is, whatever you need or want, whatever you're missing, you're already lost.

Whoever wants to win something loses all, and the one who wins is the one who has nothing to lose – if such notions can be used at all, because all our victories or defeats exist only in our own imagination.

It's happening all the time. All the time you justify yourself, make excuses for yourself. You know very well that what you want and what you do is not at all useful, right or healthy, but you want and do these things because you always find a justification for your doing. In the case of even the smallest things, you are still there in the background, you are the one supporting yourself, you give yourself the proof, assurances, justification, and that will never cease.

We praise and brag about ourselves and our achievements and victories and we want to impress others, make them envy and admire us and everything we have: our car, our house, our money, wife, husband, child.

Does your Rolex show a different time from an ordinary watch? Of course not. But it shows you are different from ordinary people, in particular it demonstrates to you, to yourself, that you're worth it. Nor is it important what you have achieved, what goals you have reached, the important thing to you is that it has also been noticed and recognised.

Most people can easily live their lives without ever tasting turtle soup or climbing to the top of the Eiffel Tower. But there are also those who don't want to be ordinary, who still want to be special, enviable, important.

You have built a fence, a perception filter around yourself, through which all things, circumstances, relationships and phenomena are analysed and judged – by your own assessment.

It's you who have solved everything for yourself and pigeonholed it, making it easier for you not to think too much about all kinds of things, so your life is plain and simple and you're ready with answers and solutions for anything – often sweeping generalisations.

'All men are pigs. All officials are malicious. All Jews should be eliminated...'

You have created this attitude all by yourself, you have identified yourself with your feelings, wishes, attitudes, opinions, assessments and imagination. You've identified yourself with your life, your relationship, your acquaintances, your family, your affairs and your assets. You may have identified yourself with your business, team, race, your own language or religion, your own people or your country.

Louis XIV said: *'I am the State!'* Hitler wrote a book entitled *My Struggle (Mein Kampf)*. In many countries we sing about how *our* fatherland is *our* happiness and pleasure.

How often people say:

'This is my baby!', 'This is my achievement, my money, my husband, my wife, my business!' or *'It belongs to me, it's mine!'* and *'I know, I need, I must have...'*

Do you belong to your parents, are you their own? Of course not.

And similarly, you don't own your achievements, your money, your husband or your wife. You have started to associate yourself with them, you see yourself together with them, but why and how should they relate to you? What kind of relationship should they have with you? It's not all yours, it's not all about you.

Even your thoughts, feelings, opinions and assessments are not yours. Absolutely everything we know, believe or think is learned, acquired, obtained from others, from somewhere read or heard, and then we have compared, combined, reordered and resubmitted it. Rarely, if at all, is something totally new created.

And once this is understood, it will soon become clear to you that there is also no need for fame or recognition. You know very well what you're worth and nobody else needs to add anything.

If you don't need recognition, it doesn't matter very much if anyone cares about you, whether you belong anywhere, whether anyone knows anything about you or notices you.

And if it doesn't matter where and how you belong or what people might think of you, then the fear and anxiety will soon fade, the need to be somehow protected or secured disappears.

Thereafter, the need for sex, food and sleep may also start to decrease, and even breathing may slow down and become easier.

Enough is enough!

'They want to make me laugh there,' said a six-year-old boy who didn't like children's shows.

And the same could also be said about a lot of other things. They always want to make us laugh, surprise or amaze us, draw our attention, make us have fun. They want to make us experience something new and special, something never experienced before: knowledge, understanding, excitement. The whole tourism business and the entertainment industry work just on this basis.

Yes, it's all possible, and interesting if you want something. It may seem to you that there is something you're lacking, and that's why you need something else – a new experience, idea or whatever it is.

Look around in any mall or shopping centre. How many things can you see that are actually necessary and inevitable in there?

Alcohol, cigarettes, cosmetics, sweets, cakes, ice creams, all kinds of snacks, soft drinks, tea, coffee, flowers, jewellery, souvenirs, carpets, magazines, books, toys, movies, TV sets, stereo systems, cameras, DVD players...

Which of these does someone actually need? All these things, all these new models and versions of things, new fashions and other kinds of stuff are actually needed only to entertain, reassure, surprise and excite. These are all remedies for the mind.

Our mind is sick, it wants and wants, more and more, but that means there's never enough. Because all these 'medicinal products' can only be used for the external signs, the manifestations, the symptoms of the disease.

They seek to satisfy the immediate desires and wants. The disease itself remains. The deeper needs will not go anywhere.

Greed and fear are said to be two basic driving forces in human society. And there's also a need for recognition: let everyone be impressed, astonished and envious!

But why? What does that give you? What need does it satisfy?

You don't have to have a place downtown with a sea view, somewhere quiet, on a hill, in the woods... And how much do you really need shoes, dresses, costumes, handbags, suits, ties, trousers, shirts, underwear, china, cars, motorcycles? Rooms, houses, land, palaces, castles? Women, men, friends, companions, servants? Respect, power, glory? Comfort, caring, condolences? Love, sex, excitement?

The same goes for news and entertainment. Do you have to watch the news every day, to constantly be aware of events around the world? Why do you need to know that somewhere a train crashed or someone divorced someone?

And why do you need so much entertainment? Why do you have to play music all the time, why do you have to watch the series, movies, shows, play games, be a fan of your favourite team...

When can I say, now this is enough, enough is enough? *Never.*

It would still be the same, with something still lacking, still wanting for more, endlessly, without an upper limit. But there is never satisfaction and insatiability remains, because there is no purpose, no final state, happiness or whatever, which actually exists.

Yet, in the name of that consumerism, forests will be cut down, plantations and fields will be planted, ever more factories and warehouses, loading containers, expanding ports and roads, cargo ships, trucks, trains, planes... And all of that in itself causes a lot of trouble.

But, here, we are talking about what this endless desire will do to us. There might be nothing wrong with it: there are always things that aren't actually necessary, why not?

This includes, for example, all works of art, poetry, literature, music, and in fact all human culture.

After all, this over-consumption also has a brighter side. As the world economy thrives, so do people's living standards. Never before has humankind been in such good health. Hundreds of millions of people can now use fresh clean water and electricity for the very first time. People have more opportunities for travelling, communicating, self-development, etc. Not to mention important technologies like computers, the internet and much more.

It's a problem only if there are no limits, if you still only want to drink beer, smoke, eat junk food, look for new excitement and then get fat, sick and stupid.

In nature there are usually limits, confines, boundaries. Just not enough resources, food, water, space, light, whatever. Or death will come before you finally get hurt or make a fool of yourself. The tree can only grow until it falls down beneath its own weight. It grows to death. The mosquito can suck blood until it explodes. It sucks to death.

A sense of natural restraint has left us, and now we can only be enticed by the pleasant or appealing. And we tempt ourselves to be foolish.

Perhaps the wise teachers and sages were right who, since ancient times, paid attention to moderation, taught people to develop mindfulness, advised them to seek peace of mind and not to react on each and every occasion.

Laozi:

*If you know it's enough,
that's enough.*

If our natural sense of restraint has been lost, we must learn to set limits, to control ourselves.

And that begins with an attentive, mindful state. Try getting used to the habit, when you are looking around a mall and you see something interesting or pleasant, of stopping for a moment, contemplating and thinking about it.

Why do I want it? Do I need that?

The wishes and wanting will not lead anywhere; they will take us away, away from comprehension, from insight and clear understanding. The worst that can happen is that you get what you want, and fulfil your wish. That should be feared and avoided if at all possible.

If the wish comes true, if you get your desire, be prepared for the worst. It's no longer possible to get out of it. The trap is already closed. You put yourself in there, into your own desire by your own intention, which you considered to be yours.

You identified yourself with your desire, built a trap and now you are there and you suffer. Because reaching your desire did not offer any final satisfaction, no eternal happiness, nor joy.

It was a way that did not lead anywhere, nor could it. That thing wasn't what you had imagined and thought about, it was just your imagination, an illusion.

Any desire or wish is immediately, from the outset, a false and flawed idea. And if it happens that, one way or another, some of your wishes are fulfilled, new wishes and desires will arise, and new mistakes, new disappointments will come. And that will continue endlessly.

Many nations have parables, fairy stories and cautionary tales of how the fulfilling of all desires with a golden egg or with someone else's support will inevitably lead to misery, catastrophe, destruction.

Understanding starts with the appreciation that you're not missing anything.

You don't need anything, you have everything, you don't need to demand or want anything, you're already there.

Laozi:

Unnamed and natural
doesn't want anything.
There is no desire,
there is silence.
There is peace in the world.

We need something only because we feel like we need something, as though we've missed or lost something. The understanding starts when you begin to realise that everything is already here, that enough is enough.

When you understand that there is no need for new excitement or rewards; that nothing or no one has to make you happy or surprise you, offer some new pleasure or experience; and that no one has to admire you or respect you.

When you realise that you don't need to impress anyone or make them envious; and also that you don't need to give anything, or make anybody laugh or be happy.

When you know you don't have to prove anything, either to yourself or to anyone else; when you don't feel you have to look like someone else, and when what they think about you doesn't matter at all.

Then you will understand that none of this necessary for being. Then you know how to be.

It's raining, somebody insults you, but why should it concern you? Why should it concern how you are?

Laozi:

Wishes bring evil.
Unease brings trouble.
Wanting brings misery.
If you know it's enough,
that's enough.

How to die

It's not an easy social conversation, but if you already alive, you could also think about how to die. And the suggestions are generally all the same – like a tree releasing its blossoms – just lightly. Yes, they were on the tree, they were part of it, they grew from it, they were its flowers. But they flourished and fell off, just easily and lightly. They went away and were gone just like anything else.

Death is just as simple and natural as birth and life. If it was, it was and when it went, it went. It's not something that should be feared or regretted. Death is not something that should threaten or intimidate anyone. You die anyway, sooner or later. As it's not an achievement or purpose, it can't be some sort of punishment or someone's revenge. Immortality can be achieved only by those who are already dead.

Of course we protect ourselves from cold and heat, rain and wind, refrain from getting hurt and avoid pain. If we're sick, if we get hurt, if we have some kind of disease, it's just our body that's sick, that got hurt, that has a disease. It doesn't have to be our concern. Of course, we'll take care of our body, treat it so it gets better, but that's all. No need to identify yourself with your body, or to feel sorry for yourself.

And of course, we can also take care not to hurt anyone else, or cause suffering to others. Just as we defend ourselves, this is how all creatures are defended. Each one has a desire to survive, to stay alive. Maybe we don't always understand and recognise each and every creature; perhaps, inevitably, we will cause suffering and death without knowing. It is also true that there is no absolute goodness, nor full release from the consequences of all our acts in this world. However, kindness and empathy, compassion and attentiveness can be developed. There's already a lot of help with this.

Sure, we have an instinct to survive. But it's not a fight, not a match. There is no need to imagine fighting it and winning, or having to save lives and avoid death at any price. You can't avoid it anyway.

There is no need to research death or to find any special reasons or explanations, meaning or purpose in it, as for life. We don't ask why the flower withered, why the leaf fell off. It doesn't even matter whether the flower was cut off and fed, or broke somehow, or fell off by itself. No grief and no regrets. All blossoms flourish and wither. All people die. There is nothing extraordinary or unprecedented, tragic or dramatic about it.

Of course, the flower could still be flourishing and things might have gone differently. All the time, things happen, all the time things can go in one direction or another. But when it has already gone one way, it has gone. Just as only a flame can fade out, only a blossom that flourishes can wither – so only one who lives can die. It is only living that gives us the chance to die.

Death doesn't teach us anything. Dying is no longer studying. Someone who is dead won't learn or do anything at all. However, one can learn and understand its inevitability, and also its instability. It's the same inevitable change as any other. Everything is changing, nothing remains. Nothing really matters or has meaning if we don't consider it important and special. And how is your death really special? Why should you be the last one to die if a catastrophe or even the end of the world should arrive?

We may be able to admit that everything is temporary and void, but it is very difficult for us to agree that we ourselves are also temporary and void. We want and we hope to always be here, without changing or disappearing anywhere. We very reluctantly tolerate the changes that take place in ourselves. We suffer because of them.

We pity ourselves. We take everything about ourselves very personally. We are stuck in our thoughts, in our imagination, in our own feelings. We get too serious about our concerns and our problems, our relationships and our attitudes.

Because if now, as a result of these feelings and sentiments, the wishes and desires appear, the cravings and affections materialise, the temptations and the will to pursue them emerge, *'for me!', 'for myself!'* – asserting the utmost importance of self – then there is no way to stop, prevent or withhold any more. Then the unstoppable downturn will begin, and there will be no more exits.

It's like a mountain river that has finally reached the edge of an abyss and transformed into a waterfall. It's like the excitement of crossing over the last boundary that has unintentionally been breached. There's nothing left that can help here, there's no way anyone can rescue or save you any more.

There will inevitably follow all kinds of hell, the incessant inconveniences and the suffering, and you will be thrown outside, into the darkness, where there will be weeping and gnashing of teeth.

You can get rid of this reason

Actually, it's all pretty scary.

Because everything you want and do, all this you want and do only for you, by yourself and for yourself. All the wishes, intentions and doings come only from someone who has created them by themselves and for themselves, but who is not really there.

The image of the self is something that doesn't have any significance for anyone else, with no connection to reality. It's something that doesn't exist, an illusion, a fiction, an imagination. And then that image requires, wants, hopes and acts. And then it suffers.

It's really pretty horrible, but you can get rid of it. Maybe you could just think about what you really want. You don't really want to get drunk or get high. You don't want sex, you don't want money, you don't want all women to love you, or all men to adore you. This is all an external, self-imagined world, it's all addiction to circumstances, just about what you see, hear, understand, feel.

In fact, what you'd really like is to be happy and satisfied, you want to feel good, you want to be joyful and free. This is your fundamental desire, purpose and aim. Everything else is just the means and the tools to achieve it.

Selfishness, self-absorption, being self-important is just a feeling, an illusion. You can get rid of this feeling or illusion, this imagined self.

Notice how feelings very quickly become personal and rather selfish. *(I feel, I like, I don't like it.) How we* very easily identify with our own feelings. *(I'm angry, I'm sad.)* Yet no feeling belongs to anyone; anyone may seem to feel something, but no one *is* the feeling.

Feelings are just what someone 'feels', maybe what they 'feel like', more like an image than something 'real', and so the feelings don't have to be taken seriously either.

It's like a game that kids play and then sometimes ask if this is still part of the game or for real.

But this illusion of oneself feeds the great and monstrous *ego:* selfishness, self-admiration, self-importance and superiority over others, plus endless self-justifications – a misconceived aristocratism, in which one considers oneself more intelligent and better in every way than anyone else, seeing mistakes and shortcomings only in others.

It is especially sad when somebody who feels superior starts ridiculing, mocking and belittling others. It's sad because derision and malice towards others will not help anyone or make anyone better, neither the person being malicious nor the one on the receiving end. It's no way to make friends, and nothing good will come from it; on the contrary, the hatred spreads.

Every contact, each relationship, every interaction is inevitably a confrontation, a collision between different people, different worlds, perceptions, expectations, wishes, deliberations, hopes, opinions, assessments and attitudes. Any relationship is inevitably a disaster.

Pirandello has described it beautifully: When I communicate with you, at least four characters interact. Because I don't communicate with you, I communicate with my imagination of you. And you will inevitably communicate with your imagination of me.

And even if we would like to improve this situation somehow and I try to communicate with you as you imagine me to imagine you, then it all would get even more hopeless.

There follows from this, however, a very important understanding. Whatever they say, no matter how they feel about you, whatever they think of you, none of it is about you.

These all are the perceptions of the speaker, they are just attitudes and opinions about you. Whether these opinions, attitudes and statements are condemning or approving, they don't need to be taken personally.

Adequate communication, understanding each other, is basically impossible.

We only admire and fear, love and hate our own imaginations.

Of course, the question may arise of whether there is any need to think, say, do or wish at all, if all we see and feel is only our perception, if it all relies only on our self-consciousness, which has no relation to reality, and which doesn't really exist. If it's all wrong, if we don't understand the reality, wouldn't it be better to give up all kinds of deliberations, desires, opinions, thoughts and deeds? They're just misleading, disturbing and upsetting both ourselves and everyone else...

There might be two ways of being or living: whether to live with all of this, to be involved, to be imprisoned in it, or to be out of it, to be free.

You may, of course, contribute, worry and wrestle, fear and rejoice, enjoy and gain, insult and disrupt, prosper and frustrate; you may be within this matrix, in this illusion, in these customs, agreements, commemorations, game rules, norms, beliefs, taking it all seriously, in a personal, heartfelt way...

But you may also be apart from it: seeing, understanding and feeling without letting it disturb you, smiling at the spectacle of it all. A clear vision and right understanding will not preclude the doing. On the contrary, it lets you do everything right, do exactly what you need to do, what needs to be done, without latching on to everything, being attached to the results, without wanting to achieve anything.

Laozi:

Who *achieves, recedes.*
When finished, just leave.
Let them think it happened by itself.

We could wake up and start living instead of playing this game. It can't be won anyway; it's hard to even stand out. You're tied to responsibilities and promises, you're indebted, you feel guilty, you're ashamed and you're scared. Of course, you can't give up on it all at once, but you can start to reduce your involvement, cheerfully, kindly, with compassion.

Knowledge does not interfere with this process, although it is not particularly necessary.

You can still admire the sunset, while at the same time knowing that the same sun is going to rise somewhere else, that it's already shining straight down on someone else's head. You just know and understand that an event isn't meant for you, that it's not taking place just for you or because of you, and that's why you don't need to be complacent, insulted or upset.

You may also celebrate someone's lottery victory, while knowing very well that this victory consisted of the small losses of many other people.

You can rejoice in a child or a beautiful young person, while naturally accepting that in a hundred years they will be reduced to dirt or ash.

But there is no particular benefit from such knowledge. Everything comes and goes away, everything is temporary, nothing is permanent, everything will change.

To be free from something is not a loss, because there was nothing to get rid of, because nothing persists.

Laozi:

The world is empty.
Like bellows.
Every move has an effect.

Five obstacles

There are five obstacles or brakes, hindrances on the way to this release. One could also call them the five stupidities or ignorances, five childish or immature things.

Ignorance also has its own causes, and conditions under which it appears. We can be stupid or unaware of many things, but if they don't relate to anything, if they don't have a chance to appear, they will remain unnoticed and no consequences will follow. As in the case of a seed, germination can start and the seed can sprout only under the right conditions, so our stupidity only becomes obvious if the right conditions exist.

A lot of this comes from thinking. What we think will come, because we create the conditions for it with our thoughts – we feed it and prepare the soil for it. And if we have stupid thoughts, in appropriate conditions they may start to grow into a pretty big, disturbing obstacle.

It's not even stupidity, it's mostly just ignorance. We haven't realised something or didn't understand – there are a lot of things we just don't know. We can't know everything and there is no need for that, but it's generally enough to understand that there is still very much we do not know and will never know.

However, we ourselves are not an obstacle to ourselves. Nobody's 'self' is greedy, contemptuous, lazy, uneasy or suspicious.

We may accidentally, by our stupidity and ignorance, allow ourselves to have these obstacles, but they don't belong to us and we're not them.

These obstacles come and go, they just need to be detected, to be noticed. It's not easy.

We don't want to see them, we hide them from ourselves, because we don't want to admit our own stupidity and misconceptions, our imprisonment and dependence.

In many cases, these obstacles become obvious through some new or different circumstances, some kind of unfamiliar situation, or in relation to reading a book or watching a movie, because of someone's random remark, or during meditation or another practice.

Living and being constantly in the same regular routine and in an environment where nothing new happens, these obstacles may not come up, and everything seems to be normal and correct. That's why we need to change something from time to time, go somewhere else, see something else, be somehow different, change the environment, the conditions. Some unexpected event or accident may prove equally valuable and necessary. Thus, we will better understand ourselves, and also notice these obstacles.

All you need to do is to detect them, take notice and then do something to eliminate them. These are serious matters. Denial or any kind of justification, or blaming, accusing or insulting other people, should be avoided. There are five of these obstacles and people usually have their own favourite, which is frequently the most hidden or, on the contrary, the most justified:

Greed – *'Yes, I want it, because I need it!'*

Contempt – *'But it is disgusting, strange, bad, evil...!'*

Laziness – *'I don't have to do anything, I'm the oldest/the youngest/the weakest/the most ill here...'*

Unrest – *'This job has to be done! If I don't do it, it won't be done!'*

Suspicion – *'Do you believe the wolf's talk...?'*

They can, of course, be named, counted and classified in various ways, but they are all with us all the time, naturally.

Let's take a closer look at them.

Greed

The first obstacle is any desire, need, greed or craving – whether for money, career or recognition, for some person or thing, car or house, woman or man; whatsoever or whoever. Also, wanting to gain power over someone, to make someone miss you, to make somebody suffer because of you, to make somebody dependent. These desires and intentions can influence everything.

Wishes and desires that seem good and right can also hinder and obstruct you. Love and respect, affection and belief may be obstacles, including affection for your teacher, student or successor, love for your parents or your child.

It may be some kind of food or drink, some substance it seems impossible to live without, like coffee or tea, alcohol, tobacco, cannabis or another addictive drug. Obviously, it may be sex and related desires.

But it may also be certain living conditions, certain standards that are either desired or, once acquired, are impossible to give up, like warm water or an internet connection.

It may also be some event in the past that you miss, some dream of the future, or someplace somewhere you'd like to be. Something that is important and necessary, which you feel you should always have: certain books, music or art collections, whatever.

It may also involve certain habits or rituals, some type of superstition, numbers or astrological signs, some kind of holy relic, a talisman, a sign, a symbol, a word, a place, a situation, a man, a tree, a holy place, a temple or a church, which seems to you essential and extremely important.

It may be a religion, belief, prejudice, principle, ideal, theory, teaching, treatment, a way of living, whatever.

Anything that you already like, anything or anyone you appreciate, might be an obstacle. Even believing in goodness and an attachment to doing good can get in your way.

All these things can hold you, get you stuck, and obstruct your clear vision and understanding.

It's like seeing everything through a beautiful, worthy filter, as though through pink or pale blue tinted glasses, or through coloured water.

It hinders, disturbs and slows you down. And it can be removed by looking at things purely and clearly, just as they are, putting aside our selves and our assessments, being detached.

Contempt

The second major obstacle is contempt, irritation, hatred, intolerance, maliciousness, reluctance. Even just considering that something or someone is weird or ridiculous, and then condemning, discouraging, disparaging. Or sniggering, smirking, taunting or humiliating someone, spreading rumours and gossip.

Contempt or intolerance is the flip side of the first obstacle, affection, and it's possible to be heavily stuck in either. It doesn't matter if you like something or you hate it. In both cases, you let irritations get to you, you collect them, you hang on to them, and you let them interfere with you.

Someone's language or dialect may seem offensive, their nationality or the colour of their skin. You may be repelled by their manners or habits, origin or hobby, religion or culture, lifestyle or addiction. You might want to intervene in someone's life because of these things, to teach them, to get that person on the right path, and not even in a malicious way but only to do good.

This contempt for someone or something may be so deep-rooted that you don't even notice it. You may even consider it natural for some nations, places, politicians or heads of state to be despised and ridiculed. The same goes for various human characteristics and tendencies.

Of course, there will always be things that we don't like, whether it's a smell or taste, phenomenon or change, person or thing, situation or event, but we don't have to stick with or engage with them, and we don't have to let them influence us. Making a decision about someone doesn't say anything about the other; it says something about you.

E. Roosevelt: *Great minds discuss ideas; average minds discuss events; small minds discuss people.*

In fact, there are very few things that should make us nervous, contemptuous, worried, agitated and disturbed, or that we need to be warned about. These are all just our own feelings, thoughts, opinions and imaginings.

Such feelings should not be shared or spread around. It doesn't help anyone or fix anything for you or anyone else. It only leads to turmoil, and you just add to the noise.

There are two important 'discoveries' that are often hard to bear, or hard to understand, and which can therefore irritate and overexcite us, which is why we want to talk about them to others, share them and proclaim them.

One is the discovery that there are differences and the second is that everything is changing. Let's take a closer look at them.

Yes, there are differences. We notice this when we meet someone or something different or special, in a way we haven't seen before, and discover that not everyone or everything is always the way we thought, believed, expected or knew. That there are other kinds of people, different opinions or knowledge, assessments or beliefs, understanding or faith, that there are other ways of life, cultures, customs, other manners and practices.

And then we talk about how it affected us, what we felt, how we were surprised, etc.

In fact, things like this shouldn't upset anyone or get them overexcited. People are different. There is no need to compare anything or anyone with your own imagination, opinions or anything at all.

You thought something, but now you've learned something else, something more, so why get upset? The cause of such irritation was simply stupidity that came from ignorance.

Talking about such discoveries, proclaiming and sharing them with others is simply the disclosure of your own stupidity. You don't need it.

The second 'important discovery' is that something has changed, that something is no longer what it was before.

It's the same stupidity. Why should everything stay the way it was when you saw it or felt it or knew it, or the way it was in your childhood or whenever?

Why be irritated, angered or offended because now it's no longer the same as before, and then insist on talking about it to all, annoying everybody in the process. It's especially stupid.

Everything is changing, nothing remains the same, and neither do you. You can't blame anyone.

One of the weirdest, but also the strongest feelings, is the desire to keep oneself clean, to be pure, to come out spotless, to clean up – both literally and figuratively. As if all around you were filthy, disgusting, dirty, and as if you were like an innocent flower in the middle of it all. It is affection for oneself, self-love, self-admiration, and getting rid of it is a true ordeal.

Many people live in a bubble like that, believing themselves to be cleaner and better, more beautiful, skilful and smarter, and that others are despicable, to be pitied; and then they constantly try to teach and improve the others.

The first two obstacles, greed and contempt, are in that sense similar, as in both cases you may imagine that something good and right should be done in order to improve the world, forgetting that this world was created and imagined by yourself. You're just stuck in your own thoughts and imagination, with your own greediness and/or contemptuousness.

So what are you going to hate, what don't you like? Your imagination? Yourself?

Yes, this obstacle may also show itself as self-hatred, self-pity, bitterness, self-deprivation. There are people who live in self-denial, complaining, while others become self-important and full of praise for themselves. In both cases there is, of course, a mistake and they are stuck.

There are countless potential examples of these first two obstacles, but perhaps the examples here are enough to help people start to notice them by themselves and discover something about them.

This contempt and denial can be released.

It's possible to realise that you were just reacting against something or someone. You may realise that being against something or someone doesn't mean anything, so nothing will change. You're just going to get worked up, overheated and full of yourself, trying to press forward and push your own opinions.

It's like boiling water under constant pressure – you can't see anything clearly for the steam.

To release it, remove the heat and the pressure; peace will help – just take everything lightly. You don't have to fight, you don't have to explain, and you don't have to prove anything. You can be free and joyful, at ease and without worry.

Weak people take revenge, strong people forgive, intelligent people ignore.

Laziness

The third barrier is laziness, boredom, fatigue, distraction, indifference, negligence, letting go. You don't care, you're not interested. Everything seems pointless, useless, unnecessary, a waste. As with previous obstacles, such laziness may not always be clearly noticeable. A person may seem on the outside to be very straightforward, careful and decent, but in his home, car or garage there is dirt and disorder.

It is quite typical to create an external impression, while letting the inner confusion become overwhelming. Of the justifications, as usual, there is no shortage. *(Ah, no one will see, these are my things, it's my home, I can live as I want. What's the point of cleaning it up, it will soon be a mess again?)*

Unfortunately, with this kind of negligence, you create obstacles and humiliate yourself. The inner confusion and filth will not allow you to focus on important things, to clearly understand or see them properly. A little of it – the laziness and carelessness that you consider to be your own personal and internal affair – may easily come out and manifest elsewhere and in another, totally unforeseen manner.

Neglecting your surroundings will inevitably affect other areas. You soon begin to neglect other things, because it feels more convenient. Many of these small things may eventually become one great barrage of carelessness.

And again, it may be very difficult to notice this, because everything starts with very little things. *(Why make the bed in the morning? You're going to mess it up tonight.)* And that's how it goes.

If you don't move your body, it's going to be powerless and you won't be able to use it. If you don't care about your mind, thoughts and feelings, then they are going to be useless, you won't be able to cope with them either.

Your living space will be covered with dust, because you can't be bothered to deal with it, but at the same time your consciousness, your mind and your thoughts will become dusty as well, without you noticing or knowing.

Carelessness about oneself leads inevitably to carelessness about everything. And soon you give up on everything; you don't do anything any more, everything seems meaningless and useless, and the depression, fatigue and distraction keep growing.

It's like an inexorably spreading, dirty, rotting pond, where you can't see through the mud any more. It's very easy to sink into this sticky, warm, comfortable mud, for that requires no effort at all.

The feeling that nothing makes sense is a similar illusion, based on the mistaken idea that everything has a point, a purpose.

Continuous and sharpened attention will help give you the necessary energy to conquer this.

Unrest

The fourth obstacle is vain turmoil, anxiety, fuss, worrying; wanting to intervene, control, keep an eye on someone or something, do everything; wanting to change something, get somewhere, get away from somewhere, get something done, get ready. Also fear and uncertainty that there will not be enough, that you cannot cope, will not cope. Wanting to explain, express your opinion, teach someone, put someone in their place, tell everyone something, make the final decision, punish someone, expel them, give them the axe.

Everything seems to move very fast. There's no proper time or place for anything, all is in progress, nothing gets done.

Often, it comes with a series of repeatedly circling stories that you tell yourself, with which you torture and upset yourself, including guilt about something, and there is no peace to be found.

Again, such restlessness may not always appear and not in every respect. For instance, there may be anxiety for one's child but a relaxed attitude or even indifference about work, and sometimes it's quite the opposite.

Such unrest or dissatisfaction may arise quietly and go unnoticed. Thoughts wander uneasily, never stopping or concentrating on anything, as if they want something all the time, never satisfied. Sometimes the worry is about what has already happened, sometimes it's anxiety about upcoming events. It may also be an anxious feeling that somewhere some important event is happening right now and you don't know anything about it, and you have to immediately make contact, communicate, watch the news, etc.

Such an anxiety disorder can lead to an insanity if you don't notice it at the right time and nothing is done about it. In a moderate form, it's very common.

It pays to observe your moods and the movements of your mind, to notice how they sometimes revolve around a totally unhelpful question. You can learn a lot about it, understand what is happening and how unrest can occur. Noticing these patterns, paying attention to them, understanding... And let them go.

They're just your own thoughts, nothing else. They don't belong to you or to anyone. They have no value, you don't have to keep them. You hurt yourself if you make them more important, if you associate yourself with them and speak about them. You don't need that.

It's like incessant waves on the surface of the water that don't let you clearly see what's underneath.

To get rid of unrest, it is best to take a vacation, calm down, abandon, dismantle. The final release can only come through deep inner peace.

Suspicion

The fifth and last obstacle in this list is suspicion, doubtfulness, distrust, scepticism. This is one of the most powerful obstacles. Nothing is believed, no one is trusted, nothing is sure.

(Everyone wants to let me down, everyone cheats and lies, everywhere there are secret plans and conspiracies. All officials are corrupted, all politicians are cheating, there's something hidden behind the curtain, nothing's ever what it seems. We are treated like playthings, just fools naively trusting and believing; instead, be wise, maintain a sober mind and doubt everything.)

This often leads to a sense of superiority and ridiculing of these 'fools', which in turn amplifies the attitude.

Such incessant doubt, suspicion and mistrust inhibit and paralyse all kinds of action and cooperation. If you are always afraid that someone will let you down or steal something from you, if you can't trust your closest friends and colleagues, if you have to keep an eye on everything, you'll get to a point where important and necessary things come to a standstill, and new thoughts and ideas are not even acted on, because pessimism has taken hold. You are sure that nothing's going to work out anyway.

Such doubt and suspicion get in the way of sincerity, trust and respect for other people, different views and beliefs. It means not believing, being unable to see or understand when something is really done or offered simply by good hearts, when someone helped and supported without striving for any kind of benefit, without wanting anything in return. The less clear are the motives behind requests from other people, the more they are suspected and mistrusted.

It can lead to a kind of persecution complex, paranoid thinking and incessant fears.

This obstacle also includes doubt in oneself, un-necessary self-analysis, hesitation and uncertainty.

(Am I still on the right track, do I still fit in, am I being counted, what do they think about me?)

It may lead to the desire to avoid any kind of communication, to be hidden, concealed, withdrawn, away from everything. In this situation, serious communication problems, severe introversion and isolation may develop.

The greatest mistake is the fear of making mistakes, of being wrong, because of a lack of self-confidence. And all of this is the use of mind as an obstacle.

It's like poisoned water in which nothing can grow, flourish or bear fruit.

Against that, trust, friendliness, conviction, confidence, sincere commitment are recommended.

* * *

In order to remove all these obstacles, the most useful assistant is full attention and awareness. A sharp concentration of attention, focusing fully and precisely on what is happening now, what is just taking place, what is immediately at hand. With such mindfulness, we can simply and plainly see through everything, peacefully, without surprise, without thinking or analysing.

Such a sharpness of consciousness, such full awareness, should be constant in a functioning state of mind.

The second good assistant is pure and clear wisdom. Not just thinking that wanders around and is aimed at objects, but rather an intuition, an understanding, like a flashlight in a dark room.

First of all comes the realisation of what it is, then the vision and understanding of what makes it up. Then the 'self' and everything related to it will be removed, then there will be insight and understanding that everything just comes and goes and does not happen to anyone in particular.

The highest level, however, has been achieved if there is nothing more in mind, if consciousness is totally empty and independent, completely open and aware. Then there's no longer the need for a teacher.

The third important assistant is power, force, might. It can be brought immediately to the moment, to the present; it puts energy into all kinds of doing, and brings the whole into everything. This power is indispensable to the effort to be constantly in the moment, to be present, right here and now. It will also remove and neutralise the five obstacles that we have talked about.

Then it will be clear. We don't have to become anyone, we don't have to change anything, somehow move or develop, progress or achieve.

We can be just as we are.

Do what you want

Before every action, before every move, there is the intent, the will, the willingness to do it, to say it.

Every action has consequences. It's *karma*, but there's nothing mystical about it. Karma is an act, together with all the resulting consequences.

You can't say, *'I didn't mean to say that!'* Yes, you did. You said that. Maybe you didn't want the consequences that followed, and that's a pretty big difference.

The same goes for everything, every activity and event. Every sentence, every word is an act. Every move, every glance, smile or smirk is already an act. Every breath, every step is a deliberate action and has consequences.

Everything we do should be done on purpose, not accidentally, randomly or by chance. We can achieve this by paying full attention to everything we are doing, by being mindful of our actions.

In fact, every thought is already an act. Before something is planned it is already in the mind, in your thoughts, at least for a moment.

Every idea changes the world. Every thought has consequences, karma. Thoughts are as real as any other things, events or phenomena. Everything comes from consciousness, from mind, and everything has consequences.

The mind creates what it thinks. Do what you want, but then really want to do what you do. Have the thought, acknowledge it, and then be completely present in what is just now being done, what is just going to be done, down to the most pivotal moves, down to the smallest things, always, all the time, constantly, in every situation.

Of course it is a complicated effort initially; of course, no one will manage this immediately or easily, but it can be attained.

That is why it's important to develop, practise, train yourself so that the mind does not react wildly and randomly to the prevailing stimulus, does not lose its grip and scatter, but is able to make the right choices and decisions, to see and understand the nature and structure of things, and avoid doing anything unintentionally or accidentally.

Only the undeveloped mind is weak, helpless, dependent on circumstances, incentives, illusions, perceptions.

It would be better to make sure that you really want what you do – really, in the sense that you understand it and are aware of it.

Do what you want, but then really *want* to do what you are doing.

Nothing to do

Actually, there is no need to suffer – you can be free, everything is all right.

We are very weak. Almost every circumstance can knock us off track – someone says something, we discover something, see or hear something, whatever. We are dependent on circumstances.

The cause of all this suffering and disturbance is very tiny and void, a small and soft thing. It doesn't even need to be thoroughly discussed; there's no need to worry about it, no need to pay even the slightest attention to it.

All these disagreements, concerns, troubles and suffering do not have to touch you personally. Look at them from a distance and you can see much more easily and clearly that they have no connection to you. Get up, step out, don't worry about yourself, don't get involved, don't take anything personally, don't get upset.

The rain doesn't mean to upset you; there's no need to feel anxious about it. Only you can let yourself be affected; it's just your decision and your choice, whether you let something get to you or not, whether it's going to affect you or not. Only you can do that, and only you can avoid that.

There's nothing to do and there's no need to do anything anyway. If you leave yourself out, there's no one who can get hurt. If you're not there, no one can harm you, hurt you or insult you. That's how simple it is.

If something irritates you, disturbs you, makes you nervous, or something unpleasant – or pleasant – happens, you don't have to do anything or react in any way. It just doesn't matter.

You can notice, recognise – and forget. You're not responsible, it's not about you, not because of you. You don't always have to react, you don't have to do everything right in every situation, to want something or to change or improve things, or get upset at all.

Any kind of affection, taking something too seriously, being involved, is addiction. Anger and hatred are addictions, as are all kinds of feelings, needs, wishes and desires. Nothing has to touch you personally, you don't have to associate yourself with it. You know, you recognise – and let go.

In the world you see and feel, there are all kinds of phenomena, people, animals, trees, clouds, etc., but they are not you, not part of your personality, and they have no connection with you. All the world lives and exists the way it is – let it be.

Wanting is what's going to ruin everything. If you want someone that doesn't want you, if you want to go somewhere you're not invited, it's going to upset you, it hurts. Wrong desires, enforcing your will, living within your wishes and hopes – this is the main cause of all suffering, inconvenience and trouble.

Any desire or wish is a bad idea from the very beginning. Whoever wants or craves something is already in trouble, lacking something, not satisfied, not content.

Contentedness is not indifference, nor is it agreeing with everything or approving everything. You are satisfied with yourself first. You are satisfied with who and how you are; you don't let anything or anyone disturb you, and you don't wish for anything. You don't put yourself out into this world, you don't think about it or judge any of it.

So what is right then? There is no need to want or hope anything. Let them want, let them wait and hope, let them call you up. Just show up, be visible, be open. Let the chances and opportunities come if they want to come.

There is no need to rule out or despise anything. It's sufficient just to look, pay attention, be interested. There is no need to wish or want anything – everything is possible anyway.

Do what you need to do, fulfil your normal duties, be present and useful, without being pushed anywhere, without competing with anyone. You can still see everything and feel and communicate as you like, in your own way, with your own thoughts and judgements, why not?

You can also help *'win friends and influence people'*, by recognition and thanks, praising and admiring, and paying special attention to their individual personalities. One of the most powerful influencers is to say or write a person's name, because everyone loves to hear and see their name. Name is the most direct link to self.

Such ways of influencing people are not completely honest and are also readily obvious, which is why they are not particularly advised. By the way, the name and personality are closely linked, and in the case of a serious spiritual turning point or 'rebirth', a new name is often given.

None of this has any connection with you, anyway. No matter how much you are recognised, no one really cares about your wishes or your feelings. No one appreciates or misses you, no one threatens you, no one hates you, no one has anything to do with you. You don't have to worry about it at all.

There is nothing to do.

Laozi:

If there's no wisdom,
there are no worries.

How far are yes and no?
What's good and what's bad?
What to fear and what to regret?

Pointlessly, endlessly.

Joy and party in spring.
People have all come out.
I'm just quiet
like a kid without laughs,
indifferently, irreversibly.

Everyone has so much,
I don't have anything,
confused, stupid.

Everyone is in the light,

I'm only dim.
Everyone is so smart,
I'm only worriless
like a teetering wave.

Everybody knows what they're doing,
I'm only primitive,
I'm only different.

I love my nourishing mother.

Matrix

You have built the world yourself, imagined and constructed it, built a matrix where you can behave and react, where you can anger, offend, deceive, gain, enjoy, rejoice, all through you. You're looking for it all, you find and get it all, you need it yourself, not the others.

You are free to think that you are the most important thing, that your feelings, thoughts, opinions and views are right, that you do everything right, that you're the one who everyone should be counting on. You made your tiny soft thing hard and important with your self-consciousness, and you're proud of it. You made yourself upset and excited. It seemed so natural, it let you live, it was something that you could really be sure of. *(Who can you trust if not yourself? You are the one who knows!)*

Without such self-confidence, without believing in ourselves, we might go crazy, jump off the roof.

In fact, doubting this kind of belief and trust in some way is very revolutionary, even dangerous, and no one likes it. Every time someone's personality is touched in this way, irritation and anxiety are immediately provoked. *(Aren't I right?)*

In order to simplify life, we often make generalisations and simplifications, to avoid having something new to invent, to investigate, to find out all over again. Put everything in its place, classified by some kind of external attribute, and it's going to make life easier. Mostly, the generalisations are disparaging. *(All blondes are stupid! All men only cheat and lie!)*

On the other hand, we may also believe that, for instance, Catholics or Buddhists are somehow better people or that dark eyes give testimony of some inner passion. One may think that good cultivation or noble birth carries with it a certain level of trustworthiness or consider someone to be particularly attractive if born under certain astrological sign. You can believe anything.

But if it becomes clear that it's not true, if someone doesn't meet those expectations, if somebody is just not like that, then you will feel deceived, betrayed.

And the blame is placed, of course, on the one who was placed on a pedestal, who was considered better than he or she really was. There are even rare cases of people seeking revenge or hurting someone for this reason, despite the fact that they were the ones who were wrong.

In actual fact, you had the mistaken idea, you believed some signs or characteristics that you had categorised, but now you accuse the other person and annoy them because they weren't as you had thought and imagined.

And what are they guilty of? Worst of all, your personality tends to get caught up in all this.

Because you must be always right, even if your mistakes are obvious.

But just try drawing someone's attention to this, try telling someone something like this, try explaining what is happening. Anger and offence are guaranteed. Nobody likes their self-confidence being questioned in any way.

We have grown so attached to our own judgements, our convictions, within our matrix, and regard them as ourselves.

All of this will be taken personally.

How dare he be different from how I had thought!

But there's nothing to do.

We also talk about how we often suffer because other people change.

Why don't you love me any more?

Well, he or she loves you or doesn't love you, but that matters only to you. You care about it, you miss it, but who are you?

Maybe you've changed. You're not the same person you were ten years ago; even yesterday you weren't exactly who you are today.

Who is the one who suffers and feels miserable? A lot of what happened in the past and meant a lot to you has now changed, time has gone on, and now you have other things that are important to you. You've changed, your thoughts and opinions have changed, you're not the one you used to be.

But who are you really, you could ask. And you will see that there is no real 'you' at all. There never has been and never will be.

All your opinions, thoughts, assessments and values change and that's natural. You are the author of your thoughts, opinions, prejudices and assessments; you have created them yourself.

They're not you, you don't have to think of them as yourself, it's just your creation, your story that you've been telling yourself all this time, something else you've imagined that can be dismissed.

Every sentence that starts with the words

'But I...',
'But for me...',
'Why me...',

inevitably contains a false, erroneous idea.

Your world view, principles, opinions and intentions, all your wishes and pleasures consist solely of your own imaginings, which you have acquired, learned, read, heard or seen and allowed into yourself, then integrated into your personality.

It's the fence, the matrix you've put up around yourself, through which you see and evaluate everything, make decisions and act. Or, using another metaphor, it's a cage, built by yourself. This is an illusion, part of your imagination, and has no connection with reality.

Yet you decide, you act, you want, purely on the basis of what you think and appreciate. And then you wonder why the results of your decisions and actions are not what you thought and anticipated.

The reason is quite obvious: you considered your opinions, thoughts and assessments to be real things, you believed you were right.

How do you get rid of it? It's very simple – just remove that matrix, that cage, that fence. Let it go.

Look straight, purely and clearly. Don't think about anyone or anything, don't judge anything. There is nothing to do. It just stirs you up, tricks you, distorts your perception and doesn't let you see clearly.

Why is it any of your business what someone thinks? Why should someone's opinion, or anything at all, upset you? It needn't touch you in any way. And similarly, it doesn't matter what you're feeling.

Who cares about your views or what you think about? If no one is interested, there's no need to talk about it. And even if someone was interested, then it would probably only be to confirm their own opinions and thoughts, to show that they were right, that they were thinking the same way. (Sometimes this is also called friendship.)

If what you see, read or hear doesn't fit in with what you imagined and thought, it means only that your imagination and opinions don't match what you see, read or hear, that's all.

There is nothing wrong in what you see and hear, it's just what you see and hear, but it doesn't have to touch you in any way. You don't have to rage in anger, turn it around or fix it, you don't have to teach anyone, or make something clear. But you may calmly think about it and redress or rectify your own imagination and opinions.

Many times it has been said,

'Change yourself – and the world will change'.

In terms of living and being alive, change is very important. Life is changing. Everything changes.

It would be even better to give up all of these ideas. You are not your feelings or thoughts, imagination or opinions – they don't belong to you, they're not yours.

You don't really need to count on them or hold on to them – they're not worth anything. Keeping them alive creates only suffering.

In fact, we have installed this program for ourselves thanks to culture, education and experience.

We have thus shaped our world picture, our world view, and we are using it to live and to be. From time to time, we still download and install new versions, get more knowledge, acquire new experiences.

Alas, we tend to forget that the picture we see, this world picture, is just a picture but not the world itself. It's just a user's screenshot, the user interface that came with the program. Of course, we have made this picture more convenient and more beautiful, changed the colours, added more features.

But this picture has little to do with the real world, with real life. It's just a model, an approximation.

We may already understand this when we notice that many of its functions simply don't work. We may realise that the whole program, meant to help us live and exist, was written using the wrong expectations and assumptions.

But we still believe it's right and adequate, and we're capable of getting into a fight with someone to defend our world view. We may even be willing to die for it.

Even worse, we consider it to be our own; we may even think that we ourselves *are* the self-image, the world picture, this world view.

Schopenhauer wrote a whole book about it: *The World as Will and Representation.*

In fact, there is still an option for living with it, seeing through the tricks, through all these illusions, looking at it all just like a user interface, and feeling much more real joy, actually.

That's the choice: whether to take the blue or the red pill...

Suffering and inconvenience are the friction, the cuts and bruises, getting hurt when your matrix collides with different circumstances that are not consistent with your perceptions, expectations or opinions.

That's what makes you miserable, that's what causes the unrest.

It's not you suffering, but your imagination. You don't have to pay attention to your imagination, you can just let it be. It doesn't really have any significance.

Well, you were imagining something – very nice – but then it turned out that you imagined it wrong – so what?

It's not necessary to get locked into every one of your own imaginings, to interact with it or to take it personally, to confront it, to be offended because of it, or even to do anything about it. It doesn't matter at all. You can get rid of it – it doesn't mean anything, nor does it have to hurt anyone.

Similarly, there is no need to be anywhere else, away from it all, to worry or rejoice because of something in the past or the future, to gnash your teeth over past happenings or brag about old victories, to live in fear of future horrors or wait impatiently for great happiness.

You can think or fear, hope or worry and plan whatever you like, but actually everything goes differently than how you thought, hoped or planned.

You don't need that either. Don't put yourself into your thoughts, your intentions, your concerns, your fears and your hopes.

All moods, all things, all people, all changes and events are temporary, they come and go, they never offer full satisfaction and they don't belong to you or to anyone else.

Events and circumstances just happen, come together, come up, and there's no way we can control them. However, we can control how we adopt them, how they affect us.

Being in the moment

Everything that has ever happened is over now. Maybe somebody remembers, someone could have done something about it somehow, something may be left of it, but there's no longer anything we can do about it. It's over. There's no way to change it, no need to worry about it, it's gone and it doesn't exist any more.

It is true, of course, that we do not have many means to think about and organise our lives other than what we are, what we have already experienced and understood, all those past experiences and lessons, *the path* we've passed and left behind.

And of course there really were important experiences and insights, events and happenings, so endless and often incomprehensible. What matters is how we understand them now. How and why we were there, who we influenced and in what way, and whether it meant something. This kind of understanding can profoundly change things. How we are now, this is important.

Whatever was, was – you can't change it any more, you can only let it go, forgive, get rid of it. Why cry over spilt milk? There's no need to hold on to it – it's already gone, there's no more. And you don't yet have what may come, what can come. Everything can come, but at the moment it's only in our imagination, the idea, the dream or the fear.

You can let go of the past and the future. These are illusions, perceptions, opinions, attitudes. There may be something to do, something to change right here and now. It's the only moment that's real.

But this current moment is also very temporary: it will not stay, it cannot be held, it has never been before and will never come again.

Therefore, there is no need to immediately react to what is happening right now, to the actual event, the situation, the person or whatever. It changes anyway, goes by, disappears, grows up, gets old, dies.

And similarly, all kind of moods, feelings, thoughts, wishes and opinions will also pass.

You can see and know how everything has come, where everything is going, without having any thoughts or ideas about it. You can see and find out how things happen right now.

You notice something, you see, hear or feel something, very accurately, very carefully and in a very focused way, as it is, neither from your point of view nor from anyone else's.

And then you understand and realise how and why it's happening just now, just here. You understand this in a very natural way, purely, immediately. You understand the causes, the situations and the conditions that created it, and you also understand why and how it will disappear again. It doesn't matter whether it's a matter of substance or something in your own mind or imagination. It could be a message or a sight you saw, someone's action or words, a memory or an idea. Everything arises and disappears, everything is temporary, dependent on the conditions, and we can't control or stop that.

But if our own relationships, attitudes and perceptions become involved with what we are seeing, with what we have just started to understand, it will immediately violate this clear understanding; miscellaneous feelings will arise, thoughts will start to run wild, and suffering will emerge.

Something can only be genuinely and truly, clearly and perfectly freely understood if we have left ourselves out, when we have stepped out of it; only when our attention and consciousness are sufficiently clear, undiluted, sharp and precise will we really understand. Let go, reject your own wishes, intentions, thoughts, imaginings, opinions or assessments so they do not create any feelings or relationships.

Not *'I hear it'*, but just *'there is hearing of it'*; not *'my knee hurts'*, but just *'there's a pain in the knee'*; not *'I remember'* but just *'there's a memory'*. It's not all about you. This is clear vision, clear sense and understanding.

Then the suffering and the inconvenience will also cease, then we will see, perceive and understand truly and clearly.

Sometimes it's also called enlightenment or awakening.

What needs to be done is what needs to be done. Breathe, eat, sleep, take everyday actions, no more. More can be done, but it's not needed.

Laozi:

The needed has to be done.
The missing is useful.

Getting rid of selfishness offers the chance to see the world clearly, purely, at the source data level where nothing happens personally, neither to you nor to anyone else, where everything just is and just happens. Getting rid of the overarching knowledge lets one see and know all at once, as if in a flash of light, allows one to realise everything, as it really is, directly.

It may be difficult to understand initially. It still tends to appear that there is some kind of meaning or significance, an idea, purpose or reason, as if the values and meanings of everything could or should be judged. But no, this is not the case, neither for oneself nor for anyone else; these are all just our own thoughts, imaginings and feelings. They have no connection with reality.

And at the same time you realise that you are no more than others or, to be more specific, no more important.

There is no reasonable justification for why you should have bigger, newer, more beautiful, more expensive, more fancy possessions. Why should you get somewhere faster, earlier, before anyone else? Why you should be better than others?

When Albert Schweitzer was asked why he always travelled in second class, he used to say: *'There is no third...'*

Survival is not the most important thing to fight for. Being is not a fight; the struggle for life is just a myth, a fantasy. Anyway, all living creatures die and only those who live can die. The self-preservation instinct is universal in nature; wanting to be alive is natural, but it is not selfishness.

In the case of a human being, however, the self-preservation instinct together with ignorance emerges as selfishness, the *'self'*, looking for something else, more rejoicing, more happiness. Alas, it will never end, it cannot be satisfied.

No need to fight, nor to harm anyone; you can just be now, be here, just easily, lightly and freely.

There's a very good mental practice – do something right, do something necessary, just like that, without anyone seeing it, noticing or recognising it. Has something fallen on to the pavement? Pick it up and put it to one side. An empty plastic bag or cup left somewhere? Take it away and put it in its proper place. Someone's talking in a tough voice, bothering people, provoking a fight? Don't get involved, don't add more fuel – you'll make it worse. It's not all about you; it all goes away, disappears, and is resolved naturally.

The mess is spotted by everyone. But if everything is all right, nothing's going to bother you, and no one's going to pay much attention. No one notices, no one recognises such small actions or non-actions, no one thanks or praises you for that.

Laozi:

Let them think it happened by itself.

These are all minor things, but the world is getting cleaner and better. Actions speak louder than words.

And what's particularly important is that you feel better in yourself. You didn't get mad or offended because of seeing something disturbing; you removed the source of alarm or irritation, you didn't intervene, you let it go so no one else would get upset about it.

Everything is possible

Nothing needs to be done. It's good if you have no arguments with yourself, no inner complaining voice, if you don't have to explain or prove anything, either to others or to yourself, if you don't have to do anything at all. Everything is the way it seems to you.

You can always ask in every situation, for every chance, every offer: why do I need it, why should I want to?

And thus you always see everything better, more accurately and more clearly. Just keep your own self, your intentions and desires out of it.

Your *'I'* doesn't disappear anywhere – you can keep using it; it's also good, and it can be useful too. You can still love and appreciate yourself, but if you know it's really a trick, an illusion, you can use it with much less worry, more easily and lightly.

You're free of it; you're no better or worse than others; you don't have to prove anything, explain anything; you're not forced into anything, you're free. Like when you disengage the clutch and let the car roll freely without the engine.

You can get out of this matrix, this cage, let go of it; you can see the world without any categorisation, without giving any ratings or valuations.

Yes, it's a feeling, but it's just a feeling, so let it be felt. I'm not the feeling; the feeling doesn't belong to me.

It just seems to me that I feel that feeling, I recognise it. I know it, it's a familiar feeling; maybe I use it or maybe I don't use it; let it go, no matter. But I'm not involved with it.

And it's the same with all things. Nothing belongs to me.

I can't say, *'it's me'*. I don't feel like that, it was just a temporary design, a construction, an illusion, a myth that can be surrendered.

It is likely, by the way, that such an illusion of one's own self is specific only to human beings; the dog, for example, doesn't have it. The dog is not worried about how he looks or what impression he leaves, but for a human being, the personality overshadows the world and prevents it being seen as it really is.

In Pavlov's dog, the saliva begins to flow as soon as the bell rings, because the dog remembers and links these two things, as he has experienced the connection.

Yet there is normally no connection between a bell and food. The dog experienced this connection, so it is now a reality for the dog and he reacts accordingly. The more times the experience is repeated, the more sure he is of it. When the bell rings but no food comes, the dog is just a little confused.

In the case of a man, this situation is worse because his 'self' comes into play right away. When the bell rings but no food comes, he feels like he's been deceived, betrayed. He starts complaining and making a fuss, he starts fighting and demanding his rights, telling everyone about the outrage he has experienced, as if he has been personally insulted, as if this thing has been done especially to him, for him personally.

Unfortunately, people take things like that very personally. They believe that there is some sort of regularity to events, some kind of legitimacy, some eternal truths and relationships. *(If you have a good education, you get a good job, good salary...)* And if that doesn't happen, they are insulted, annoyed, personally hurt.

We put our own self into every relationship, stirring ourselves into it. People are blind and foolish in that sense, seeing everything as it seems to themselves, unable to take things just as they are, freely and naturally.

We are living and can only live in this world because of others, thanks to other people and thanks to all living beings. And therefore we have no reason to hope or ask for anything, no right to demand anything, no reason to expect anything at all. No one promised us anything, and everything we receive is a donation.

Life is a gift. Nothing is guaranteed but death.

The smarter way is just to be open, and try to understand other kinds of people, things, situations, events, different attitudes and points of view, without irritation, without becoming involved in them. *(Perhaps you might even learn something and develop...)*

But the most reasonable way would be to let everything live and be just as you live and be. Why can't everything be the way it is? Why should you intervene? Why does that touch you?

Laozi:

Open your mouth,
argue everywhere
– only worries.

All kinds of reactions, irritations, confusion, anger and taking offence are signs of weakness. They show dependence on circumstances and overestimation of oneself. They demonstrate a lack of confidence, selfishness, foolishness and living in illusions.

You shouldn't demonstrate these things to everyone. You shouldn't immediately react, comment, express your opinion, get irritated or angry, argue and thereby inform everyone around you of your foolishness and ignorance.

Any overreaction will only give testimony to your low level of understanding, lack of enlightenment and imprisonment in your own thoughts.

You should rather be ashamed and conceal such feelings and reactions. There is no benefit to anyone, and the joy of such outbursts is only shared by those who behave in the same way and have similar opinions, thoughts and attitudes, and who thus gain support.

We all want something, but we should think about whether we really need it. If you don't know what you want, then you don't get what you didn't know you wanted. But why would you want anything? It doesn't matter.

Of course, people want and need something all the time, for all kinds of reasons. And of course this can be used and abused for all kinds of purposes.

In our current cultural tradition, perhaps the most essential need seems to be the need for recognition, to feel oneself to be necessary, to be considered valuable.

But something remains behind these defilements, the darkness and the stupidity, behind selfishness, illusions and desires. There remains a feeling or knowledge of the nature of mind and the true nature of things, their original state, the possibility of really being outside conditions and incentives, being free and independent of them, the option to see and live, for real. There remains a reminder of paradise.

Continuous dissatisfaction with existence, with all these surprises, wonders, sufferings, deliberations and inconveniences, inevitably reminds us of this paradise. All of them can reassure and comfort, by teaching us that reality is not like these temporary enjoyments, not like dreams or cravings that come and go like clouds. Yes, these clouds obscure the clear skies, pure light, sun and stars, but knowledge of that light and the stars will no longer disappear.

Clarity and understanding are available right here and right now, totally separate from your thoughts, opinions, imagination, your wishes and desires. Clarity and understanding are always there and never disappear. Action can only be taken immediately, right now and here, not in the past or in the future or somewhere else. And there is more: seeing and feeling everything the way it all is, without attributing any meaning to it or giving assessments.

In every very first sense, in every first moment of perception or experience, we are in the garden of Eden, in innocence, in paradise. We see, we wonder and understand, like children, purely, truly, directly. However, in the next moment our own 'self' enters the game, and immediately, on the basis of our previous experience, from our own knowledge, it gives its assessments – you should like it or not like it, and other kinds of judgement – and it ruins everything again.

In general, we are not particularly interested in other people. Politely and moderately, of course, we ask them, 'How are you?' and that's all.

What we really care is how they feel about us, how important we are to them, how important they are to our relationships.

And the same goes for everything. The relationship is all-important – how it affects us, what it means for us, as if nothing could exist without a relationship, without assessments, without giving opinions.

Is it possible to get rid of it; is it possible to see and understand things, people, events and relationships without having to involve yourself in person, without it having to mean something to you? Yes, that's possible.

It doesn't mean much to you, what anyone else thinks about something. Then why should somebody else get to know what you think about? What's the difference?

You're not special, you don't need to consider yourself important, you don't have to yearn for this, worry about it or suffer.

Yes, it's true that you've never been exactly as you are right now, and you never will be again; you're the only you, unique, that's all right. Neither will there ever be a grain of sand or snowflake, sunset or cloud, dream or love that is not unique.

Everything is changing constantly – think about it. Why should anyone consider a cloud or a sand grain somewhat special or important? Why should you consider yourself a special personality? It doesn't matter.

Intellect is just a property of the mind, like all the doors of the mind – hearing, touching, seeing, tasting, smelling. In our cultural context, rationality is highly overrated compared with developing the mind in general. When intelligence is being developed, at school and elsewhere, the mind will start to demand from it more and new exciting experiences. *('Learn well, find a career, earn money, buy stuff, go travel, collect excitement... The more intelligent and clever you are, the more eloquently you can offer it all to your mind...')*

Intellect and mind can be used in a much better way, by taming, muting, staunching, diverting, developing this unbearable mind; by not letting it react so easily to everything, not paying attention to its childish wishes and cravings.

Alas, the intellect is always carefully developed, the mind not so much, and therefore the need for excitement will never be satisfied; new and more stimulating sources of excitement are always needed. The undeveloped, childish mind will never be satisfied.

But there is a way forward.

There's a difference

Thoughts and moods can change for very minor reasons. Someone came, someone went away, someone looked, someone said something. Seeing someone, noticing something – sounds, music, a familiar smell, some small change, whatever – and now the mood changes, thoughts and understanding change.

We are dependent on circumstances, inevitably and involuntarily. Where are you, where have you arrived, what's going on around you, who's near you? It all affects us, it all makes a difference.

Landing can be heavy or light – landing like cats do on their paws, we can land smoothly – and every landing has its own consequences, just like every other event.

You always land somewhere you haven't been before, somewhere new; it may be somewhere you used to be, but now you're going to land there again and it's not the same. Nothing's going to be the same and you're not the same person any more, and everything starts again, with all the consequences.

Actually, there's always a difference. Nothing keeps repeating, every situation is new, every moment is the only one.

You've never felt like this before, as you feel right now, and you'll never get to feel like this again, and nor can anyone else. Nothing will be repeated, and this will also make a difference.

But if there's always a difference, if things keep changing, which is right and better, happiness or joyfulness? They're both going to happen to someone, to you, to me, to whoever.

It's clear that there can be no universal happiness or joyfulness, and that it's not possible because our selfishness enters the game immediately, and we are already in the game without noticing.

We can rejoice, at all times, always – there's nothing special about it. Something good happened or you succeeded, you saw or heard something beautiful, understood something, and you felt better, you felt joy. But happiness – it seems to be something eternally desirable and unreachable...

That's the way it is. Joyfulness is a feeling that may be felt, that may come. You can feel it, you can rejoice when it comes, at any point, everywhere, always. Joy cannot be wanted, joy cannot be claimed or hoped for, it cannot be desired. The feeling of pleasure is very real, undeniable. You either rejoice, you feel joy, or you don't.

Happiness, however, is about wanting something, longing for something, wanting to be happy, wanting to become happy, and that's something else. Happiness is a condition that is desired, imagined, the dream of something that is not present. There is no connection with reality or actuality.

Of course, actions have consequences, who can deny it? If there were no consequences or results, you wouldn't even imagine them. Why do we do something, do anything? To make something happen, so it will have a consequence. And there's nothing mystical about it. There is no need to start talking about any *karma* or destiny right now.

If a foolish animal, an untamed mind, draws your cart, you can get into all kinds of situations, both pleasant and unpleasant. There's nothing you can do about it. The seed has already been sown, the cards have already been dealt, and now you need to accept the fruits that have grown and play with the cards you have in your hand. No need to think about whether you are lucky or fortunate. Use the options you have in your hand and don't worry about what you don't have.

If the mind is clear and developed, the consequences will also follow clearly and directly like a shadow that you will never leave behind. But if the mind is distracted, then the consequences will be faint and unpredictable.

Mind can be developed

A wild horse may be nice to look at, but no good will come from her, no benefits. It's the same story with the mind. We may admire someone's despair and rage, suffering and tears in books, on the stage or in films, but in real life we would rather avoid such situations. Rather, we hope and expect to have a balanced attitude to life and to hostile emotions.

Like an untamed, untrained and unharnessed wild animal, the mind may unexpectedly rear up, wander off and make trouble more often than it brings benefits. That's why we need to train, teach and develop the mind, put it to good use, give it a purpose and a job to do.

Knowing the right instructions and understanding them is not enough. Benefits only come from their actual use. There are a lot of teachings and books about mind development, and from these one can acquire a thorough knowledge and understand how important, right and necessary things like this can be. But there are no benefits from such knowledge and understanding if they are not actually used.

The smoker, for instance, may well understand and realise that giving up the habit is a really good idea and the right thing to do, but if he doesn't actually do it, the understanding is no use to him.

You can read a lot of instructive books, listen to lectures, study all kinds of things; you can understand good recommendations and advice, but if they are not applied, they won't be useful. Many good recommendations on developing the mind have already been given, some of them thousands of years ago.

Skills like swimming cannot be learned from books, and similarly there is no benefit from reading literature about meditation. You have to go into the water, you need to start practising.

Every time the mind is fond of something, gives attention to something, or is stuck in something, a divide arises – subject and object, observer and observed, perceiver and perceived. Without objects, without incentives, there is nothing to be done, there is nothing to deal with; therefore, the mind is constantly looking for new stimuli, objects to get attached to, things to play with, wandering around to see and experience these incentives, seemingly coming from outside.

The mind separates itself from the rest, wants to be 'itself', in opposition, creating for itself the illusion of a subject and an object, as if this is really happening.

But the experience is one – there are no two sides, experiencer and experience. Experience, experiencer and experienced are one and the same; there is no difference.

The cause of all suffering and inconvenience is the separation of the self from the world, the universe. This is the illusion of what is outside of oneself; it is not understanding that everything is one, that there is no separation. Understanding starts with knowing that there is no separate 'self'.

If you're already one with nature and with everything, you won't be surprised any more; no admiration, no hate, no craving will arise. Consciousness is common to everyone anyway – call it universal mind, unified consciousness, or whatever you like.

Laozi:

Clarity and peace organise all.

If the mind can only react to a stimulus, it doesn't even know anything else, it doesn't even want anything different. It can't be calm, it switches the TV on, plays music. If the mind doesn't have enough incentives, it will be bored and will go onto social networks to see who is there, who has posted something in the meantime, who has commented, who has liked. The mind wants to be social and communicate, to be familiar with everything, to be sure it hasn't missed anything...

In fact, the mind is afraid of its own thoughts; it doesn't want to be unusable so that thoughts go restlessly round in circles, overwhelmed with some irritating situation, memory or prevailing problem; the mind wants to get away from all this.

But it can't do it in any other way than by disrupting these disturbing thoughts, adding a different stimulus, leading thoughts and attention elsewhere, escaping from the existing situation, pulling away from whatever trouble the mind is in.

Of course it's a cheap fraud. That's how a child can be reassured, but we don't have access to this option – it all comes back anyway, inevitably.

Trying to cheat the mind by distracting its attention will not help anyone, nor will it take them anywhere.

Just as the most natural state of water is a flat surface, so the most natural state of mind is a peaceful one. Only a flat water surface can be seen through; only a peaceful mind can perceive the world adequately, clearly, without the noise of its thoughts and wishes.

Achieving peace of mind is one of the main objectives and goals of developing the mind – to control and tame the mind so that it does not constantly demand more and more incentives.

Laozi:

Hurrying and chasing make mess.
Expensive goods drive insane.

Peace of mind is a natural condition, but if it is not developed, if it is not experienced or felt, it may instead be feared. Rather, the uneasy mind is considered normal and a peaceful mind somehow weird:

'How can you be so calm?'

When people start approaching a calm state of mind they may experience surprise, they may flinch, for some it brings them to tears, some begin to laugh... it feels so special.

We commonly recognise two natural states of consciousness: being awake and sleeping. While we are awake, we are aware of what is happening around us, and we are also aware of what our mind is doing, thinking and feeling. While there are no conscious stimuli during sleep, the mind can wander freely and dream.

But during sleep there is yet another state of consciousness – deep, dreamless sleep, when the mind is silent, totally empty of all kinds of movements, thoughts and feelings.

In the same way, what if it were also possible for the mind to be empty from time to time during the daytime, to be empty and at rest, aware only of itself? That would then be the fourth state of consciousness, which is also very natural and necessary.

During the awake state of consciousness, we can afford to remain peaceful and quiet, meditating, without worrying about anything. There are various kinds of methods and techniques that will help us to do so, that bring the mind into a condition in which it is possible to reach knowledge and understanding in a different way, through the experience of pure consciousness.

There are many other ways and means to change consciousness, either deliberately or unintentionally, accidentally. One of the most common is the use of alcohol and other substances, but consciousness can also be changed by sounds, rhythm, colours, shapes, light, smells, words, touch, feelings and more. But also under hypnosis, by some unexpected event, a tragic accident, falling desperately in love, someone's death, deep despair.

These means can also be useful, if used with awareness. As simple methods used without understanding, without the necessary awareness, they have no special benefits. Altering the state of consciousness and using the capabilities that emerge is a special art that can be learned and developed.

It is very important to be mindful in this regard. There's no need to get oneself out of nowhere, to transfer to different planes of existence. You can stay in control, you can feel and know everything that's happening.

Letting go, losing control, forgetting, giving up is always possible and sometimes even right and necessary – it may happen, but it doesn't have to.

If you can't control yourself, or be aware of everything you do – every move, step, breath – then what can you do at all? If you don't have clarity, how can you understand anything? If you don't know what you want, how can you want something? If you're anxious, worried, stressed, if you're rushing, struggling, seeking, if you need anything, if you have any kind of desire, wish, belief, insistence, hope for something, then what can you see?

Trying to control thoughts and feelings is actually useless. The main goal is not to control them, but rather to be free from their control.

Just notice them, let them appear and disappear, like everything else.

R. Kipling:

If you can dream – and not make dreams your master;
If you can think – and not make thoughts your aim...

What is enlightenment?

There is a common description of enlightenment: If you are sitting all the time in a dark room, you don't know anything about light or 'enlightenment'. You have never seen it. Nobody ever told you about it. The darkness is normal for you. You can live in darkness, you can act in darkness, you are familiar with darkness, no problem.

Of course, you have to learn first how to live and act in that darkness, how to find necessary things, how to use them, etc. But as your knowledge and abilities develop, you can manage quite well.

Even if someone tells you that you are living in total darkness, or declare that actually there is light, and enlightenment too, you probably don't care.

You may think that you don't need anything more; you may think that you're settled, living quite comfortably and everything is going smoothly anyway.

Perhaps only if you are confronted with some kind of suffering, discomfort, inconvenience, pain, sickness, sadness, bad luck, etc., will you start to rethink or maybe even search for some way out of the current situation, looking for some kind of 'enlightenment'.

And then you may notice something, for a very brief moment, somewhere, somehow.

You may hear something extraordinary and start to understand something new and different. Maybe somebody tells you something and you may discover in those words something much deeper.

In any case, these are like glimpses of something else.

But from this very moment, you are sure that there is a light or at least something different, something more. You are now convinced that you are able to open your eyes, to see that light, to reach for it.

You may even feel that you are now already enlightened, and you may also believe yourself to be somehow better or higher than others. This can be the first mistake.

It's not full enlightenment yet, of course. From now on you are just beginning to discover full enlightenment; you can now really start to move towards this light. It may be a long and hard road, difficult and long-term work. But you know the right direction at last, and that's the point.

Here you may make another mistake. The light you've seen may be so attractive for you that you start to investigate the light instead of yourself. There is nothing to investigate as far as the light is concerned. The light is the same all the time. The light is not changing.

Only you are changing. Your ability to see and to recognise the light may change. You may see and understand enlightenment better or worse. The key is inside you, not in the properties of the light.

People frequently stumble upon such things, start to research and investigate various light properties in various textbooks, in various teachings, with different teachers and techniques, etc. It's useless.

The light is the same with any teacher. Only the pathways towards enlightenment may differ – and these are purely technical issues. How to breathe in and out, how to sit and what to eat. These are just formal characteristics of the way.

Even enlightenment itself is just a word, void of all meaning. We can call it enlightenment or awakening. We can call it the Truth of Buddha or Dharma. These all mean nothing and they all mean the same.

The description above is a common way to explain so-called enlightenment, and is surely true. But this is only part of the truth.

Actually, there is nothing to discover, there is no lightness or enlightenment at all. In fact, there is only darkness. And the darkness where you are sitting is created by yourself.

You, by yourself, built this dark room around yourself. You are covered by yourself, you are sitting in yourself.

You, by yourself, cannot see anything but yourself. This dark room is actually yourself and nothing more.

Lightness is just as natural and normal as darkness appears to be, but in fact darkness is something artificial, created and built up by the environment, by society, by human relations, by educational development, etc. This is what society expects from us.

This is what society calls personality, a unique person, yourself, your incomparable and special values, your credibility, all your skills and abilities, etc. You are covered by all of that.

From your very childhood you can see only these things and nothing more. And you are proud of these things around you, because you feel yourself to be a valuable and necessary part of society.

You don't care about some abstract light or spiritual enlightenment. You are happy and satisfied with yourself, in yourself.

Yet the light is still discoverable. The way out of darkness is already here. You need only *dis-cover*, remove the cover, yourself. You don't need it any more.

Come out. Look around. Let the sunshine in. And then, in broad daylight, you can see that the darkness didn't really exist.

The cover around you, yourself, was just a myth, just a story you were told by yourself and others. It was not a real thing. It was just an imaginary, yet useful, tool in society.

After *dis-covering* this cover, called 'self', you are actually still able to act in society just as before.

Nobody will even notice any change.

The peculiarity of humans

Why are we so different to other living beings, and yet we breathe, eat and reproduce the way they do, being a part of nature, the animal kingdom, the mammals? We have the same heart, liver, spleen, lungs, blood vessels, limbs, bones and muscles as many other animals, yet we are considerably different from them.

We have trains and ships, cars and planes, hotels and malls, restaurants and beauty salons, temples and cathedrals, poetry and novels, operas and tragedies, libraries and the internet, communications satellites, and many more things that animals don't have. Why is that, and how did it become so?

At least one thing is sure – human culture can emerge, exist and evolve only in a human environment, in a society. Culture, customs, language and literacy do not come by birth alone: they are not inherited, they must be acquired, they have to be learned.

If a newborn human child cannot be among humans at the right time, he or she will never become a true person and may not even start walking like a human, not to mention talking and thinking. The stories of Mowgli and Tarzan are just fantasies.

This leads us to a somewhat paradoxical topic, neoteny, which is the delaying or slowing of the physiological or somatic development of an animal. This is a rarely occurring phenomenon in which the development of the organism stops at an early stage, but maturity is nevertheless achieved.

Some insects, for instance, remain in larval form, but yet multiply. Some amphibians also do so. But among mammals, humans are the only species in which this phenomenon occurs.

Our genome is almost identical to chimpanzees, but our appearance is totally different. Our skin has as many hair follicles as an ape, but they don't all develop. We remain bare and pale in comparison.

Simply put, neoteny means, in our case, that a newborn infant looks like a large premature monkey embryo – bare, whitish, helpless – and will remain like this for a period, only very slowly advancing and growing. The brakes are on.

After ten years or so, the human child starts maturing at last, but will still need another ten years to fully develop social skills. Without proper care, teaching, assisting and raising, this creature cannot develop into a real person.

Self-reliance, which is a natural and necessary attribute for all living animals, in order to find food, to avoid threats, to multiply, is genetically determined and instinctive.

But over the course of the long-term development of a human child, it's scope expands dramatically; the natural process of self-realisation is amplified, enlarged, prioritised. The child is admired and praised immediately, from the beginning, whenever the slightest development is achieved: when they can say their first words, tie their own shoe laces, and so on.

And the same goes for expressions of *'me,'* and *'myself!'* – words that encompass the natural self-reliance of a little person – *'It's me! It's mine! – My father! My mom! My home!'*

Involuntarily and inevitably, the child develops selfishness, prioritisation and appreciation of self, taking most things personally, egotism, arrogance and superiority, together with various perceptions and opinions, beliefs and attitudes, desires and deliberations, all of which together are called personality.

The personality wants and demands, it has wishes and needs, it is insulted and angered, desires and despises, is manipulating and doubting. It is nervous and uneasy, it wants to get revenge, it can be mean, jealous and stingy. The personality needs reassurance, somewhere to belong, recognition and respect. It needs something to achieve, something to say, some way to flourish. It fears and regrets, rejoices and enjoys, decides and makes, assesses and compares and puts everything in its place. The personality is important, it's special, it's unique.

Of course, this is not to say that such selfishness or personality is wrong, useless, unnecessary and over-arching. On the contrary, this is exactly what has given us all these achievements, all these ships and planes, poems and novels.

Unless personality had been brought into the game, all the inventions and discoveries in the history of humanity would have been left undone, and we would still just be sitting in a cave.

Thanks to this pivotal development, when this sense of self became so well developed, this self-differentiation so important, it began to manifest itself in many ways – fire, the manufacture of tools, eventually leading us to educate, build towns, create empires, but alas, also to wage wars, to sow ruin.

Obviously, our peculiarity – the stalled somatic development, or neoteny – has lasted for too short a time compared to our natural history, so we haven't yet begun to use the resulting opportunities more purposefully.

Sometimes it seems as if we need more deepening and peace of mind, then again it seems that there is a need to intensify our progress and achievements.

In this book, we have emphasised the necessity of deepening and peace of mind, and the illusion of personality – precisely as a counterweight to excessive materialism and the cult of achievement.

But if this selfishness, this overwhelming egotism in a person inevitably arises and emerges, then the question remains as to how to understand it, and whether and how to use it.

It will, in any case, be accompanied by inconvenience and suffering, and final satisfaction will never arrive, but still...

To implement this selfishness, toiling and suffering for achievement, self-fulfilment, fame and success, to conquer and win – or, how to reduce and mitigate its effects, perhaps to get rid of it altogether?

It seems that both may be conceivable, that one shouldn't exclude the other if you're moderate and balanced.

Usually, animals go through this stage of life expediently and smoothly, without any particular personality or the importance of self-perception emerging from their natural self-reliance. In the case of domesticated animals, like dogs for example, we may notice something similar to the human personality, but this may also be our own imagination or projection.

But in our case – after a long period of childhood and youth during which we are constantly confronted with various often contradictory prohibitions and demands, punishments and recognition, and given incessant care and attention – this immature human being inevitably emerges with the self-delusion of being the most important and distinguished character in the world.

If such a confused being ever came to realise that things weren't really as they had been taught, then uncomfortable feelings might arise of having been deceived and abused, of mental anguish and torment.

This human being may spend the rest of their life trying to solve these misunderstandings, trying to cope with such suffering and get rid of these mistakes.

In most cases, a final resolution will never happen.

There is a method to get rid of this

Release is possible. You can learn to see and feel everything clearly, without taking anything personally, approaching everything calmly, with equanimity, always, everywhere, in every situation.

It is not apathy or indifference, letting go or carelessness: it is surrender from a reaction based in any way on prejudices, and it can be practised every day, at any moment, in every situation.

To do everything, you think about it, deliberately, fully conscious.

Laozi:

Who knows others, is smart.
Who knows himself, is enlightened.

Some news, someone's words, some new idea are all like the winds that can lead you occasionally in the wrong direction, but they don't mean you have to forget your original destination.

Like a butterfly that is distracted by the breeze, but is not going to give up its intent to go the right way. You don't have to give up on anything.

And then you will no longer suffer for your cravings and desires, your contempt or your fears.

You won't depend on them, you won't be their slave, there will be no more preferences, and hence freedom, release, clarity, serenity and enlightenment will come.

It's all one, no matter.

It's all good, but how to achieve it?

That is the right question and there is also an answer.

Let's go back a little bit and recap. We had problems, concerns, disagreements, troubles and suffering, and it turned out that there was a reason for all this.

We made our own life, self and personality like this, with our own ignorance and stupidity. We took everything personally, and we kept it all for ourselves.

Fortunately, we can get rid of this reason, and there is a method for doing so.

Everything must be done right, carefully, thoroughly, fully, perfectly, in the best way. Not that so far everything has been done wrong or badly, certainly not. But everything can be done much better and with more correctness, by being attentive, consistent and careful, and thereby getting rid of all inconveniences and suffering.

What's important is how

- *to view*
- *to intend*
- *to speak*
- *to act*
- *to set up life*
- *to try*
- *to understand*
- *to proceed.*

These eight things are very important and we will now look at them a bit more thoroughly.

How to view

This is one of the first things that we can learn to do more accurately – to view in a better way – and then everything looks better.

To look at everything as if you are seeing it for the first and maybe the last time, completely innocently, without being prepared, without any expectation or preference. Seeing everything the way it is, at this very moment, in just this place, without it getting to you or touching you in any way, without being disturbed or irritated, without dissent or reluctance.

Most of the things that are happening in the world have nothing to do with you. So why should you bind yourself to them? Not all you see is meant for you, it's not all done or intended for you, it doesn't all have to confuse you, make you rejoice or complain.

Let it all be, just look and see, and don't let your thoughts, opinions or assessments, your intentions and desires, your principles and beliefs interfere.

Better to sharpen and develop mind, consciousness and wisdom through what is seen and viewed. To take care that the mind doesn't wander so pointlessly or spread itself out so thinly, doesn't let itself be irritated or disturbed by any extraneous circumstances, but rather that it can see, feel and understand honestly and directly.

There's nothing you need to think about, imagine or dream of. There's no need to attach any meaning to anything or to seek such meanings. There's no need to investigate whether something is somehow valuable, useful or damaging for someone, whether it's right or wrong.

You give these assessments, you are all that, you see all this through yourself and therefore you may not be able to see very much.

It just interferes with the right view, the right sight, and you don't need it.

You are what you look at and see, hear or read. You are the view and the sight, the hearing and the reading, understanding, comprehension and influence. You're stuck with it, you're one with it.

You can view by allowing clear vision. You can listen and hear, let the silence come, always listening. You start to see and hear and start to understand what's going on. You really comprehend that you are the understanding, the hearing, the sight and that there's nothing more. You start to see and understand the whole. It doesn't matter, it's all one.

All misunderstandings, disagreements and suffering are just minor things, smaller particles of a much larger picture, a more general understanding. If you no longer oppose others or isolate yourself, if you no longer look at the little things, then when you see the whole, you are already there in all of this, in its wholeness, completeness, integrity, in a world where there are no contradictions, disagreements or suffering, no desires or wishes or needs.

The basic, complete and natural is always there, always remains; it will not disappear anywhere, nor change in any way. That's what's important, what counts, what's really going on. Isolating yourself and separating from it only misses, violates, distorts, obscures the whole, stops you seeing what is real.

There's no need to fight what is happening naturally and inevitably, of course, like ageing or death. You're getting old and you will die anyway. Why should you suffer for that, and fight it? As if being young is somehow better or more true, as if death is somehow worse than life. These are just delusions.

They can't be avoided. There's nothing unfair or false about it, you don't need to take offence or worry, you don't have to get upset, you don't have to take these things personally, you don't have to suffer for them. But you can see and view them more accurately and deeply.

The wind blows and the sea makes waves. The air moves faster than water and there is friction at the surface where they meet that creates foam and waves. We don't see the wind or the sea, we only see the waves on the surface.

And in the same way we see and perceive oscillations and waves, vibration and changes everywhere. Everything is changing, vibrating and oscillating, but we may not see or know anything about everything in which these waves, oscillations, vibrations and changes occur.

We do not perceive the field, but we note the changes, differences, alterations that occur in it. These movements are real for us, because these are what we see and feel.

We see and perceive the manifestations, phenomena and events occurring on the surface of consciousness, coming through the gates of consciousness.

They are like gusts of wind. They inevitably influence our already existing perceptions, experiences and opinions and thus create a variety of thoughts, wishes and intentions.

They're like waves, like foam on the water. We live in these waves, in these surface-to-air ventures, in that foam; we react to it, engage with it, and it can seem to be the only reality.

The waves, however, are only temporary phenomena; they come and go, emerge and disappear as a result of random movements of the wind and are not particularly important.

There's no need to take them seriously, to deal with them, to respond to them.

No need to do anything about any obvious fact, to start struggling, to think about it, to judge, to fight, to be annoyed. It all flows, rises and sinks, comes and goes.

Of course, you can play with things like that, like toys; you can argue and quarrel as usual. At a certain age we lose interest in toys and in playing with them, and we understand their superficiality and uselessness.

Similarly, you can see, realise and understand how vain and childish it is to argue with someone about a little wave or get into a fight over it.

At a deeper level there is much, much more; you can see and feel, be and understand more fully, and thus understand more accurately.

Deeper reality is much more persistent and much more important.

Laozi:

The depth opens to an abyss.

All this can be said and understood in many ways. Ultimate truth can be described as having no signs or characteristics.

We can talk about the absolute, the unified field, or anything else. It may be noted that energy does not appear or disappear but changes its state, or that everything is energy.

Einstein said it particularly beautifully:

$$E = mc^2.$$

Everything is changing, nothing is permanent. Everything that comes, also goes; everything that arises, disappears. Time gives everything and takes it all. It's all one.

At some point, such words may seem too lame, even stupid.

Laozi:

The right word seems wrong.

Yes, you can view in the right way and thereby see right. This way of viewing can be exercised and learned and can be used continuously, all the time.

To that end, attention, care and continuity are needed.

How to intend

If you have already started to look in a better way and see through the temporary ripples to the real depths, to the more persistent nature of things, then you can start to plan.

Every intention is always preceded by an idea, and every thought has a reason to emerge, whether it is some kind of sensation or perception, the sight or sound of something, a smell or an idea that forms the intent to make this particular action.

It can all take place in a moment, totally unknowingly and unintentionally. You see a favourite chocolate bar on the shelf and it's already in your basket, without you knowing about your perceptions, thoughts or intentions.

Such involuntary and unintended impulses can be better realised at the same store when there is no hurry.

You walk easily between the shelves and when your glance stops at one or another interesting item, you watch instead your own thoughts and feelings.

You may stop and let these feelings and thoughts become clearer, let them sink to the bottom, understand their deepest causes and sources. And then walk on quietly.

This kind of exercise can be repeated in many different situations, until the mind starts to watch itself much more closely and no longer just lets itself be tempted, not only with food or other goods, but at all, with everything.

You can always ask yourself what you really need it for, whether it's money, career, recognition, attention or whatever.

You will also find out how rarely something really needs to be done at all, how little there is that you need to worry about, or think about. And that's how you learn to do better.

In fact, intentions, desires and wishes may not be noticed at all, if you already have the right view and seeing. For most people, desire tends to be self-assertive, relatively overarching and unnecessary, not taking you anywhere, but rather making you want something even more, and that's how you keep endlessly going round in circles.

Laozi:

If you know it's enough, that's enough.

The story with your good intentions is somewhat different. You may have very good thoughts and plans, but in the end it still turns out that someone was hurt, someone had to suffer because of you, you were bad and evil. (According to an old saying, the path to hell is paved with good intentions...)

Indeed, it is not enough to simply try to refrain from hatred and evil, and avoid causing pain and suffering. Deeper and more thorough sentiment is needed, and this can also be developed.

It is possible to reach deep, true and boundless benevolence, desiring and sharing full happiness, joy and love, and all the good things that can be offered and given, like the sun, which shines on everyone without any reservations.

You can start with yourself. Simply look at yourself, kindly and clearly, and wish yourself well. So you say in your thoughts:

'May I always and everywhere be joyful and happy. May I always be safe and well. May I always be in good shape. May I always be doing fine. May I keep finding the right way and solutions. Let the good chances and opportunities come. Let me be happy with everything that happens.'

These words, of course, may be adapted and repeated in many ways. What is important is that these wishes come from the heart, sincerely and purely, like sunlight and warmth.

Then you may think of an important person, a good friend or companion, someone close to you, and tell them in your thoughts, from the heart, sincerely and purely:

'Be always and everywhere joyful and happy. Be strong and always safe and well. Stay in good shape. Always do fine. Find the right way and solutions. Let good chances and opportunities come to you. Be happy with everything that happens.'

Then you can focus on someone who you may not even know, and who doesn't care much for you. In spite of that, you think of that person and tell them in your thoughts, from the heart, sincerely and purely:

'Be always and everywhere joyful and happy. Be strong and always safe and well. Stay in good shape. Always do fine. Find the right way and solutions. Let good chances and opportunities come to you. Be happy with everything that happens.'

The next step is particularly important, to think of someone who has done something bad to you, or because of whom you have been hurt, someone who has cheated on you, humiliated and insulted you, caused you evil and harm. And you also think of them, and say from the heart, sincerely and purely, like the sun:

'Be always and everywhere joyful and happy. Be strong and always safe and well. Stay in good shape. Always do fine. Find the right way and solutions. Let good chance and opportunities come to you. Be happy with everything that happens.'

And finally you think of all your close friends and acquaintances; everyone you know, and even those you don't know, who are in your vicinity and neighbourhood; all who live in the same house, on the same street, in the same city. Think about all people, in all the nations across the world.

Think about all the living creatures, all the dogs and cats, roosters and chickens, frogs and snakes, without making any distinctions, without excluding anyone. Think about all trees and bushes, flowers and grass, mushrooms and lichens, forests and seas, rivers and lakes. Think about all creatures, whether they are visible or invisible, known or unknown, and say in your thoughts to all of them, wholeheartedly, sincerely and purely, just as the sun would allow them to feel the warmth and light:

'Be they always and everywhere joyful and happy. Be they always safe and well. Let them be fine and in good shape. Let them find the right way and solutions. Let them have good chances and opportunities. Let them be satisfied with everything that happens.'

Such exercises can be repeated daily, honestly, with deep inner conviction and certainty. That will help. It's important to intend properly.

How to speak

The third thing to pay attention to is how to speak rightly. This is about words and thoughts that are spoken, but also in writing that others may read, whether on paper or online, in an email, a post or a comment on the internet, or even with spray paint on a wall.

Today, written words and messages can spread much faster and much more widely than ever before. It is especially important to observe what you write about, what written traces you have left for others to read. These traces may never disappear.

There's no need to lie, no need to speak badly or evil of someone, no need to talk nonsense.

Neither is there any need to tell everyone or write about where you went, what you did, what you saw or heard, thought or imagined; there is no need to take pictures of yourself and to share and spread them. It was just you who went somewhere, did something, thought, imagined, so why would it interest anyone else?

Well, if someone really asks and seems interested, there's still a chance to talk, but in any case it's all over and there's not very much to talk about. There's no need to talk about what might have been or what could have happened, because it wasn't like that and it didn't happen, so it doesn't matter.

Neither do you need to talk about the things that you're worried about, what you're afraid of, what you're waiting for or what you want to happen or not happen, because it's not yet here and it doesn't matter at all.

These are just your hopes and expectations. Anyway, everything goes differently from what you expect or hope or fear. When it comes, it comes, when it happens, then we'll see, but there's no need to talk about it now, to make yourself and others nervous.

It doesn't help anyone or anything. This is all nonsense.

There's also no need to talk about what you thought about something or someone before and what you think about them now. That doesn't mean anything either, and it doesn't change anything. We think and think about something, and then we think and think differently again. Your earlier opinions or thoughts do not interest anyone. This is also just hot air.

There's no need to surprise anyone, to amaze them, to make them wonder about something. There's no need to tell anyone anything that they don't already know. Not all people need to know all things. There's no need to affect anyone with your idle talk.

Actually, you were trying to impress yourself, but why would you need to? It's just more bosh.

The less you say, the more you hear.

Laozi:

The words are in silence.

There's no need to lie. Human society is actually built on trustfulness. People believe and trust what they are told and act accordingly.

However, if society begins to spread lies and deception, when people are threatened and intimidated all the time, when people sow suspicions, insecurity is created, and people live in fear, feeling despised and hated. It all damages people's relations and ties, sows distrust, poisons consciousness. People don't know how to function properly in such an environment. Spread uncertainty and fear, and community suffers.

Lying affects everyone. If you can't tell the truth, you'd better not say anything. Every time you lie, it stays with you, stays part of you, and you can't get rid of it any more. You have to live with it, consider it, you have to remember what you told someone that was untrue. If your lie should come out, others won't trust you any more.

Worst of all is slandering and spreading defamatory stories, even when you believe these rumours, but especially of course if you know very well that they are not true.

The damage that comes with slander means it's no longer possible to make amends and it has a devastating effect on all parties, especially the slanderer themselves. An honest person should not get involved at all, nor try to correct these stories, as this would disseminate them and no one needs that.

You don't need to lie to yourself, you don't need to admire yourself, to think of yourself at all – it's all an illusion anyway. There's no need to believe everything you hear, see or read, and you don't need to start spreading it right away.

It's especially crazy when you're really speaking badly of someone or something. It doesn't matter what or whom, it doesn't matter at all, whatever the reason. It's crazy if you think someone or something is bad, and that makes you feel better. But what's worse is telling others about it, even in hints or passing comments that may be in some way ridiculous, ironic, sarcastic. It affects you right now, directly, and you can no longer take it back.

With every word you say or even think, you give out something of yourself. Even if you say something anonymously, so no one can find out who said that, and no one will ever start associating it with you – even then, you will still be linked to it.

It is you speaking. You are the one who said that, who wrote, who thought; it was your expression, your act, your decision and it affects you – directly affects you – not anyone else. Others may be affected by it, but that's their choice. You have no choice any more, you've already said it, and you can't take it back in any way. It's going to be with you now, it's going to affect you, and you know it.

But if you lose control, if you become angry, raise your voice, get upset, if you haven't learned to manage yourself and don't understand what's going on, then things will get really insane.

Behind any offensive behaviour, anger or misunderstanding, there is always a conflict between your imagination and reality. As said Prometheus: 'Jupiter, you got angry – you're not right!'

Hold on, stop, let go, bend, give way, be thankful, kind and friendly, be helpful, do the right thing. That is important.

It doesn't matter what anybody thinks of you or for that matter what you think about anything or anyone. Every time you want, wait or hope for something, always ask yourself what you need it for. It will release. Every time you want to say something, think about why you have to say that. If you have anything to say, you'd better shut up first. It's just you who wants to say that, but what do you need to say it for?

You don't need to tell anyone about what you've just heard or found out. It may not be true at all, or you may not get the message right. Things can get especially insane when you add something to it or exaggerate, blow it up or make it sound ridiculous. You don't need this at all.

You don't need to say anything to anyone, to prove anything, to explain, to make it clear. Any desire, hope or wish is not necessary at all. Needless to say, there is no need to ask for or demand anything; all is there anyway and freely available. Just look, see, be there and you'll get it. This will release all obstacles.

All you want, believe or hope, is in you. You don't have to spread it, you don't have to talk about it – it's all there anyway. Forget your ego, your self, let them go. You don't need them. No one can hurt you in any way, and you don't have to affect anyone in any way.

There are little things to get nervous about, that make people worry or suffer. People are like that. Can your worrying or suffering help them somehow or make them feel better? How is it that you are better and smarter?

In everything that's ordinary, there's nothing special. In everything that's special, there's nothing ordinary.

There are no empty words in the right speech, no evil or lies. The right speech does not achieve anything. It can be watched, and you should be careful in that regard.

How to act

The next important step to observe is how to act better and more precisely.

There is no need to harm anyone, to make any creature suffer, or to kill. There is no need to take anything away from anyone; everything can be done so that no one will be sorry, no one will suffer, and no one will miss anything.

Why do you want to kill the mosquito who is getting close to you? She only wants to eat: she is hungry. There are many ways to keep mosquitos away if they bother you. Why should she die? It's her life, so let her live.

There are a lot of situations like this. There is no need to overreact, no need to create excessive suffering, cause unnecessary problems, or make someone worry. Even talking about your own concerns and problems may prove to be a burden for the other.

We are talking here about the intentional actions we have planned ourselves and that we ourselves are aware of.

In the world, inevitably, harm and suffering are created and inevitably all living creatures will die. We may not always know who or what we may have hurt or affected by our actions, but we know very well what we do directly and intentionally.

Only for intentional actions can we learn to avoid causing unnecessary suffering and harm.

It is not necessary to take what has not been given to you, nor is it necessary to take what belongs to someone else, or even what does not belong to anyone.

Even if someone doesn't need it, maybe doesn't consider that they own it, won't remember it, won't use it, or if you think you can use it any better. You don't need it, it's not necessary.

The same goes for person-to-person relationships.

You may like someone, and you may want to communicate more closely with them, but if there's no consent, there's no need to start trying. There's no need to start investigating the reasons or the consequences.

People are different, and everyone has their own wishes and needs, their own life and their own background. You don't have to take such things personally. With the right action, the wishes of other people will be respected and nothing will be forced upon them because of your own.

Here, the right view and the right intentions are very important, because it's not always as simple and unequivocal if you aren't living the life of a hermit monk. In the normal layperson's life, situations may always occur where your absolutely right action can make someone suffer, without you knowing about it.

For example, someone can give you something, or offer it to you, but you may not know if it even belongs to them, whether they have the right to offer you that. They may believe it themselves, but maybe someone else thinks otherwise, and if you accept it, you can cause harm and suffering.

The use of money can also create confusion and cause damage. You may have money that has been given to you or that you have earned honestly, but yet the money can't be used totally freely, with your eyes closed, to buy whatever and from whoever, as damage and suffering may also result from this.

Obviously, in many spiritual communities, people try to refrain from using money and avoid closer relationships, as they may interfere with right action and disrupt sincere commitment and devotion.

Often, they dismiss all kinds of property, family and descendants, saying no to selfishness, individual benefits, wishes and desires.

If you don't want anything, you won't miss anything.

If you don't own anything, you can't lose anything; then you're free and you can devote yourself to whatever.

Laozi:

The wise wear plain fabric,
gold in heart.

But yet, even in the ordinary, everyday layperson's life, all of this can be applied.

It is possible to do the right things and act right if you are already watching and seeing properly, planning and speaking correctly.

Watching and seeing clearly will ensure that you do the right thing. And if the intentions are right and clear, there is no need to worry about any confusion or misunderstanding.

How to set up life

The next important thing is setting up your life in the right way.

We all are living our own lives and we often think:

It's just our life, it shouldn't bother anyone else, there's no need to pay attention to what others think, or think about how they are.

And that is right in some ways. But it would also be right to notice how we conduct our own life and business and how we are with others.

We don't live alone in this world: we share it with other people and other creatures, and we form relationships with them. We affect them and we communicate with them even if we don't realise it ourselves, even if we don't know them, understand them or think anything of them.

It is nice to imagine oneself as the centre of the universe and consider the rest of the world only as our own imagination, which there is no particular need to care about. Nevertheless, this world is affecting us; we are influenced by this world, and there is nothing much we can do about it.

And similarly, we impact this world ourselves and influence it. Every move, every word, glance, smile or frown changes something in the world you're in. You will be noticed, you will be counted, even if you do not notice or remark on it yourself.

If you're already living, if you're already here, then you're also responsible for yourself, and you'll inevitably have to accept all the consequences for how you live and how you are. You've created this world by yourself and for yourself.

It's all one, no matter. We start to create and influence this world right from birth.

Our first sounds make other people pay attention to us and act to take care of us, right from the start. There's nothing we can do about it.

Even just by existing, you already have a huge effect. Your existence alone has many consequences and you are therefore truly dangerous and frightening, even when you're standing still, even if you're not doing anything, not thinking anything, and nothing seems to be happening.

It's the same for everyone, and for all living creatures. The earthworm also affects the world in which it lives, the pine tree shakes its powerful head and makes us sing about it, and it's the same with everything that exists.

Maybe the mountain doesn't know that, just because it exists, the waters are flowing down its side; maybe the water doesn't know what effect it's having on this hill alone by flowing down it. It's hardly possible that the sun, the clouds or the wind could understand or perceive how important they might be to someone.

But we can understand, consider and be aware of the effect we have, because we have this option. We can arrange our lives and our way of living right, to set up our lives the right way. We can try to be and to live in such a way that less evil comes into being.

There is nothing very complicated about this, if we have already started to view, to see and intend, to speak and act in the right way.

Just look and notice everything that is not needed, that is not suitable for the right livelihood, that may harm someone, cause unnecessary suffering. We can look forward, see more, and further into the future. We can understand and notice where the consequences of our lives and livelihoods can lead, and what can happen.

We know where everything that lets us live comes from, because we create it with our work, with our own action. We can also take this further and understand what we don't see directly, but are also contributing.

If we have realised that there are no lies in the right speech, that we should not contribute to lying and cheating, then there's no need to work and make a living where people are deceived and lie to others.

There is no need to contribute to that, no matter how little or however indirectly. It will inevitably restrict you and not let you live freely.

If we have understood right intentions in the deepest sense, we will clearly see if there are no right intentions, if causing pain and suffering is actually the main goal, where making money from failure and delusion is the business. And again, there is no need to contribute to that.

There are very many things that are meant to cause pain and suffering to other creatures: arms, other means of slaughter, traps, poisons, etc. There is no need to either directly or indirectly have anything to do with them, no need to contribute to killing, injuring or torturing anyone or anything. It doesn't matter whether it's a person or some other living being: all are one anyway.

Please note that we are not talking here about all such activities being somehow bad or evil, or people being sinners, or condemning it all – oh no, far from it.

We are talking here about how to be, how to get rid of inconveniences and suffering. It is absolutely possible to be attentive and careful not to cause inconvenience and suffering to others.

You can't be free and happy if others suffer because of you.

How to try

None of the important things we have already talked about, however, are much use if there is no energy or power to launch and sustain them.

It is not enough to know how to properly view, plan, speak, act and set up your life, while not actually viewing, intending, speaking, acting or setting up your life in this way. We may have very good tools, instruments and apparatus, but if we don't switch them on, if we don't get them started and don't use them, nothing can be done with them.

All these important things have to be put to work by trying properly, with sincere commitment. For this purpose, solid willpower, desire and effort are needed.

It is the same desire and willpower that also fed our selfish goals and ambitions, spurred us on to achieve, made us hunt for recognition. We gave up those desires and intentions when we understood that the assumptions behind them were void.

But now we can apply the same energy, the same force in a much more valuable way, more appropriately, more productively and much more accurately, because we already have the right view, the right intentions, and so on.

There is no need to let this energy go to waste. It can be consolidated and directed consistently into momentum, attention and focus. It can be used to dispel the mood of fatigue and laziness, which may prove to be a very major obstacle. It's not an easy job, but it's not impossible.

To do this, you have to keep yourself alert all the time, ask yourself all the time, every day, repeatedly:

Am I still viewing right, are my intentions right, am I speaking in the right way and doing the right thing, have I properly arranged my way of life?

This work cannot be done for us by anyone else. The results of this work cannot be understood, felt or appreciated by others. We just need to do it on a daily basis in order to get anywhere.

Removing those obstacles that we have already talked about – being greedy, contemptuous, uneasy, lazy and suspicious – takes the most energy. They do not come from anywhere outside, but from within. They are inside us all the time, hidden, in a dormant state and quite still. In suitable conditions they may awaken stealthily, first distracting our attention, blurring our clear awareness, and later emerging and becoming more powerful.

When we catch these obstacles depends on what stage of our spiritual development we notice them. The first sign of danger is distracted attention, blurry focusing, drifting thoughts. This may be noticed at a very early stage, even before it has really happened – as soon as there is the smallest disorder, the tiniest deviation in focus. In this case, it is easy to return to clear focus. With long-term experience and practice, such actions will become almost automatic.

It is somewhat more troublesome when the thoughts have already gone wandering and we are distracted, awareness is lost. In this case, the loss of focus must be reversed in the same way without any blame or investigation.

The most complicated situation is when an obstacle has already taken control and we are already sinking into it. We notice that we have started dealing with some of our longings and desires, thinking bad thoughts, going over concerns or problems in our minds, we are tired or sleepy, or have started to suspect or mistrust.

There is no need to deceive or justify ourselves, as if this sinking was somehow valuable or necessary, as if it helped us analyse things in such a way as to achieve some essential and important conclusions and decisions.

On the contrary, it only shows that we were weak, we didn't try hard enough to maintain our focus, and that the obstacle had more energy and capabilities than we did.

'Dad, is it possible to do several things at once?'

'Yes, of course. For example, right now I'm talking to you, watching TV, reading the paper, listening to what mama's talking about, and I still snooze at the same time.'

Doing several things at once is not a superpower to want or aim for. This is what most of us still do all the time, automatically, so we are often in a state of confusion and nothing can be done properly.

Much more rare, more valuable and more wonderful is to focus on only one thing, one activity, one event.

One thing at a time, one activity at a time, entirely focused, so nothing interferes, nothing confuses or distracts, no other thoughts or feelings, fears or suspicions.

This can be attempted and it can be practised, by focusing on something completely insignificant, something ordinary, which does not relate at all to your feelings, thoughts or memories: focusing on the focus just for its own sake.

For example, if you can just take enough time to observe the movement of air in your nostrils, or the movement of your feet while walking, then you are already able to do much more.

With full attention, there is never anything to do or to try. It is sufficient to observe and notice what is happening now, without intention, desire or hope.

Like a cinema. You're not involved; you don't have to react, jump on the stage and get involved in it; you're just watching, without doing anything, without discouraging anything.

How to understand

Eventually, we will start to see, realise and understand how little is actually needed or essential. Nobody sees, knows or understands everything and it isn't necessary. It's enough to understand and realise important things, real things.

But it's also true that mostly we don't have time for these important things, for the facts.

In everyday life we are forced to deal with all kinds of everyday things, and if at the end of the day a free moment appears, we would rather use it to rest and switch off, and we are not interested in reality or eternity. We push such thoughts and ideas far away, out of sight.

Of course we know, and every now and then we faintly remember, that there is something more important than this day-to-day nonsense.

That there is, somewhere deep and quiet, in the depths of all our physical manifestations, personalities, opinions and assessments, work and activities, hopes and dreams, something much more persistent and much more important than all these surface-to-air ventures.

But most of the time, in order not to hear its deep and quiet humming, we muffle it. Because it disrupts and stirs.

This itch can't be scratched, the humming can't be switched off.

From time to time it emerges, kicks out and reminds us in one way or another that there is something more important than the life we live.

Somehow we also suspect that something is very wrong in our lives, but at the same time we will do anything in order not to think too much about it.

In other circumstances it quietly arises in the background, letting the eternal light shine over our temporary problems as if waiting for our dedicated attention, but when this does not appear, it goes away again.

Understanding starts with the realisation that beyond what we see, hear, know, think, there is *still something* that can't be seen or heard or in any way described, that we don't know about or think about, and can't even ask questions about in any reasonable way.

Death, Being, God, Truth, Reality, Eternity, Clarity, Dharma, Dao, Unified Field, Unified Consciousness, Transcendence...

Laozi:

> *Suitable name doesn't mean anything.*
> *Beginning has no name.*
> *Naming creates everything.*
> *Who doesn't want to, can see.*
> *Who wants to, can feel.*
> *It's one and the same.*
> *The difference is in naming.*

It can be understood. It can be perceived. We can reach it. We are born in it. We can recognise it in the bright eyes of a small child who is not yet aware of it, who is in an unconscious world, just being in their own nature, which has not yet been overshadowed by excessive self-consciousness.

The adult, however, is usually in their self-centred world, separating themselves from being, and does not want to feel it or know anything about it.

However, with persistent understanding, it is possible to relocate, open and restore it and thereby regain the initial sense of being, serenity and clarity.

Laozi:

> *Freedom gives persistence.*
> *Persistence gives understanding.*
> *Understanding gives clarity.*
> *Without a permanent understanding,*
> *we will be condemned.*
> *Persistent understanding will open up all.*

And here comes the question that is waiting for a clear and definite answer: what is most important to you, what is your true purpose, not somewhere in the future, but just here and now, at any moment?

The answer does not come easily and is not at all obvious. You need to think about it carefully and meditate.

It's a very deep question for you, and you alone. No one else can answer it for you. This is perhaps the most important issue, because life is shaped only by what you most appreciate and what is most important to you. People frequently appreciate and consider important things. Often, however, they just think and say something is important without examining it more deeply and thoroughly. Very few are actually interested in Reality or Being.

It's true, however, that we do develop over time. Some important things remain important, while others lose their priority. We need to keep this constantly in mind, and be aware of the current moment, of our existing level and capabilities.

However, if clarity is firmly in hand and the path is quite clear, then it must be followed. This does not mean working to achieve something in the future. It means complete presence here and now, an honest and sincere desire to remove and banish all illusions, all perceptions that could overshadow our clarity and aim.

This task needs to be taken on with heart, it needs to be loved, it needs to be mastered. And if this clarity is firmly united with right intention and with unconditional love, it will become one of the world's strongest forces that can overcome any situation and fate.

Now you need to be careful in this regard, not to give the achievement over to anyone else. It's your life, you're responsible for it, and no one can do it for you.

If now, at this victorious point, you abandon your clarity, your serenity, and blindly follow whoever led you to it – a spiritual leader or teacher – this can easily lead to extreme cults, fanaticism, obsessions, hatred, and even to violence. Unfortunately, this happens all too often.

Of course, you need to respect and love your teacher and dedicate yourself to them, but you don't need to adore them, you don't need to be addicted to them. It's still your life that you live in, not anybody else's. A reasonable balance must be found.

The same goes for spiritual teachings. The teachings are not the reality, but only the guides, the direction indicators. The teaching needs to be learned and applied, but there is no need to just believe it and take it as the final truth. By the way, good teachings often influence us and work unnoticed, in the background.

However, what is significant at this point is being exceptionally honest about ourselves. This does not mean perfection. On the contrary it means, among other things, honestly and sincerely noticing and acknowledging imperfections. Complete honesty towards ourselves means acknowledging ourselves just as we are, with all our mistakes and shortcomings, without hiding or fearing anything.

It may seem painful, even cruel. Very painful and shocking peculiarities may arise. It is quite unbelievable how little we know ourselves, how easily and blithely we constantly cheat and justify ourselves, how easily we give way to intriguing temptations, and cause pain and suffering to both ourselves and others.

But honest introspection is only honest introspection. We see, we notice, we recognise ourselves, very deeply, very thoroughly, perhaps very painfully, but there is no need to analyse what we see, to praise or condemn, to feel guilty or admire, and as a consequence to act in a particular way. Do not, for example, start to blame or justify your parents or your friends or whatever.

This immense honesty with oneself wipes out all the imaginations and illusions. Honesty itself also shows, among other things, what we are actually capable of, and what serious obstacles may arise. You see yourself naked, completely defenceless, fearful, weak, helpless – very real, as you are.

And it frightens you when you understand what a villain you can be, how disgusting, timid, mean and suspicious, how weak, insane and evil you really are.

It's all of your selfishness, your inner nature, your *'me'* that ever came up and that you learned to hide carefully, to suppress, to conceal from both others and yourself.

This understanding doesn't make you better, nor does it give you any reason to humiliate or persecute yourself. Everyone is like this; you are no different, no better or worse. You're just starting to see, you're just starting to understand what you haven't yet seen or understood, for the most part.

But once again, don't analyse – just see, understand, take notice. Your true nature is just another fact like anything else.

It is possible to deal with your fair share of daily life and day-to-day experiences, while at the same time new events, knowledge and experience will come to light, bringing up something new.

And what is more, only when you have achieved full respect for yourself can you be honest with others.

Laozi:

Who knows others is smart.
Who knows himself is enlightened.
Who conquers others is strong.
Who conquers himself is mighty.

And then it's worth watching yourself. Enlightenment doesn't make anyone better or more perfect. This is one of the common misconceptions.

Right understanding, seeing clearly, is just about understanding and clear vision, nothing else. How anyone uses it is another matter.

Enlightenment just happens, it comes, it comes as a gift. It cannot be desired or claimed, its coming cannot be foreseen. But if it comes, it will be instantaneous.

There is no such thing as partial or gradual enlightenment. Well, maybe sometimes there can be something a little like that: a glimpse of enlightenment, momentary flashes, or slightly longer ones. These are really signs that something may be starting to happen. Sometimes they surprise and even startle us.

So what is happening now? Am I going crazy?

It might seem a bit like that.

Even when real enlightenment comes, it may not stay. A day or two, maybe a few more days, and then it may disappear again.

Many everyday events, among other things, can dispel it very easily. Therefore, it is recommended that we seek enlightenment while alone, with as little confusion and distraction as possible.

But it will always come back, because it has already been experienced. You know it, and you know how to be like that, so it can happen again. It no longer comes unexpectedly, like the first time. But yes, you will recognise it from the first time. If there remains any doubt, then it wasn't the real thing.

It's very hard to describe. And it's not the sort of thing we want to announce. Sure, it is a great pleasure. The pleasure, in particular, of so many concerns and problems falling away at the same time, of realising that the best things in life aren't things.

Some say it's more like letting something go than gaining something. As if a shadow is lifted, a cover removed, a curtain flung aside and clarity enters. Some say that, in fact, it's within everyone already, always, except that it's not usually seen, not realised or understood.

You understand how irrelevant and senseless were all your wishes, demands and needs, desires and hates. You know that in reality there's no point to where you live, what you do. You lose interest in a lot of things that used to excite and interest you before. No need for news, no need for recognition or attention. You're with yourself, completely, really. You get immersed in it. You flow with it. You realise you're one with everything, with totality. What happens is what happens; what happens, the way it goes, actually, is all one.

And it's a pleasure. The joy of unity, contentment with everything, while at the same time, perhaps, being completely alone.

Laozi:

No proximity, no distance.
No avail, no harm.
No value, no worthlessness.
This is true worth in the world.

How to proceed

There's not much left to say; almost everything has already been said.

Of course, anyone can live and enjoy life as they wish, nobody forbids it. You can enjoy wealth, power and glory, and everything that comes with it. Don't worry, you don't have to bother yourself with anything. You can just be, and live freely, without causing any further problems, or changing anything yet. Everything can be, and nothing needs to be done.

There are no instructions or commandments, and nothing is forbidden here. If there is anything to show here, perhaps it is only that in addition to the achievement of wealth, power and glory, there are also more important things in this world.

How anyone sees or understands this is up to them.

But in case anyone is interested in how to proceed, then we should consider it here. It doesn't matter whether you're enlightened or not. The way to proceed is the same. And the most important thing is to continue as you have been doing up to now. There is no need to fix or change what has already helped, what works for you. Unless you've actually stopped, it doesn't matter how slowly you move on. If you already use mind exercises, meditation techniques, yoga or whatever, it's very reasonable to keep using these tools.

Meditation is the first thing to remember, of course, but it should not be overestimated. This is not a universal remedy to treat all inconveniences, to solve all problems, certainly not. Nor is it the only sure way to achieve enlightenment.

But neither should the value of meditation be underestimated. The experience alone of this state of consciousness, this presence, makes it possible to feel and understand in a different way, much more deeply and clearly than in an ordinary state of consciousness.

Time spent in meditation is very valuable, particularly when practised daily, at least twice, in the morning and in the evening.

It doesn't even matter which technique you use. There are dozens to choose from. In fact, there may be hundreds, but ultimately, all of them can still get you where you need to be. It would be good, of course, if there is someone to teach and instruct you. Should there be a chance to choose, surely mind development should be learned from a trustworthy teacher, but if a teacher really is nowhere to be found, then books or internet resources can also be used.

However, it is important not to start inventing or combining methods after reading or hearing something about them, or adapting them by yourself, experimenting. These are still very powerful tools and their unskilled use may prove dangerous and cause serious harm.

If there is anything in particular worth suggesting, it would be that the simplest and most accessible focus is on something ordinary, common and totally insignificant: for instance, your own breathing. Just organise circumstances so that nothing and no one can interfere or disturb you for a period of time. Then just sit on a chair or on whatever you want, and watch closely how the air moves in and out, through your nostrils, as if this is the most important event in the universe. You're just watching it, just this, all the time, long term. You are not important, nor is the air. It is important to keep this air movement steady and close, and hold the long-term feeling or perception, in such a way that all other thoughts and feelings are gently removed, dissolved and slowly disappear.

It is being, being in, being in an immediate sense of being. It is a very deep experience that is not comparable to any kind of knowledge that can be read and learned from books or heard from others.

But meditation alone is not enough. There must also be deeper understanding and comprehension. Step back, view and explore yourself, ask the deepest questions about your thoughts, your stories and opinions, their conclusions, and remove the last false and overarching thoughts, ideas and opinions.

Now, in the silence of it, in the depths of consciousness, in pure knowledge, there is the readiness for instant realisation, immediate understanding.

And in the end there is still quiet thinking. It is an art that tends to be forgotten – to think in peace and silence over a single sentence or thought, and let it open into deeper meaning and understanding. With such reflection we can overcome the boundaries of ordinary thinking and logic and indeed discover the unfamiliar.

There is no need to analyse anything, no need to disappear into it in any way. Rather, keep it, be with it in peace and silence, and let its meaning spread and grow. Then bring it back to the surface of consciousness and be in silence with it again. And so on, many times, again and again.

We have had a lot of thoughts here. You can take another look at them.

Laozi:

Suitable way doesn't lead anywhere.
Suitable name doesn't mean anything.
Beginning has no name.
Naming creates everything.
Who doesn't want to, can see.
Who wants to, can feel.
It's one and the same.
The difference is in naming.
Together the depth is seen.
The depth opens to an abyss.

Bibliography

Ajahn Jayasaro. Stillness Flowing: The Life and Teachings of Ajahn Chah. Panyaprateep Foundation, 2017. ISBN: 978-616-7930-09-1

Anthony Markwell. Truly Understanding the Teachings of the Buddha: A comprehensive guide to insight meditation. https://www.facebook.com/anthony.markwell. 796

Buddhadāsa Bhikkhu. Handbook for Mankind. Thammasapa & Bunluentham Institution, 2008. ISBN: 978-6160303335

Buddhadāsa Bhikkhu. No Religion. Buddhadharma Meditation Center; 3rd edition, 1993. ISBN: 974-89647-3-6

Printed in Great Britain
by Amazon